PRAISE FOR *WHAT ARE YOU WAITING FOR?*

A tear-jerking page-turner, this book is simply spectacular. Implementing the Law of Attraction and the "T" Chart, brilliant. I give Nancy West a 40/40 on equipping college graduates with a guideline for living a more authentic and fulfilling life. On the weapons range, that's an expert marksman.

Avrie Welton, Second Lieutenant
Graduate of West Point, United States Military Academy

In Nancy West's book, "What Are You Waiting For? You Don't Have 9 Lives!" through the eyes of the wise and clever, Coco, a tuxedo cat, she shares insightful stories, provides guidance mixed with humor, and messages about working through fear and life's up and downs, while not letting it diminish our authentic talents, our purpose, and our beliefs. This book is bound to be a go-to resource for up-and-coming talent to begin to understand the laws of the universe and how they apply to your personal and professional lives.

Dave Ciliberto
Adjunct Instructor at Cornell University

"What Are You Waiting For? You Don't have 9 Lives!" is so cleverly written and in such a fun and light way that makes it easy for the reader, especially recent graduates, to understand how we can help ourselves and "Become More." It is uplifting and inspirational and by the end, we all wish we could have a "Coco" to help us on our personal and professional journey.

Maureen McCarthy
Director at MMC Training and Consulting

With a smile on my face, a tear in my eye and a hopeful joy in my heart, Coco's "lives" are the perfect metaphor for all of us as we face and traverse the challenges of life. Seeking, finding, enjoying, loving, losing, recovering, and ultimately deciding to take responsibility for our own happiness and being.

Coco's wisdom is profound, and yet so obvious if we "mere humans" would just allow ourselves to accept our emotions and fears, seek out, and attract people and solutions that allow us to Believe, Seek, and Do! Whatever challenges life hands us, it comes down to saying "Says who?" and deciding and acting to make things different. Even though short term pain (investment) may be required, the outcome is ALWAYS preferable to remaining stuck and settling.

As the Professor was able to demonstrate to his audience and his production crew, through Coco's lives, we all have the power to love ourselves and each other, overcome our differences, and attain our goals. What are we waiting for?

Steve Shap
Road Scholars International

Nancy West's "What Are You Waiting For? You Don't Have 9 Lives!" starts as a simple story of a woman (Mama) adopting a kitten (Coco), and grows to take on a life of its own—or actually 9 lives. Relationships with our pets appear simple, but in truth, are far from simple. They can be the key to finding happiness, and as Mama learns when she, with Coco's help, begins planning her own happiness strategy. West's work is an inspirational page turner for those who want to take control of their lives.

Peter Zekert
Independent Training Facilitator

What a wonderful, endearing story! A creative blend of friendly feline affirmations amidst the dealings of self doubts and criticisms from society. Thank you for sharing the journey!

Lisa Miller
Owner at Miller's Specialty Products, Inc.

How clever of the author to anchor the message of the power of a positive perspective and the belief in one's capacity to persevere and succeed in the story of a wise cat's nine lives. Coco's story is a metaphor for living the life of our true selves, and it is a wake-up call that time is precious—what are you waiting for?

Marilou Jasnoch
Education Consultant

What are You Waiting For? is the *Who Moved My Cheese* of today. Intended for recent graduates entering the workforce, Nancy's book puts a spin on the traditional "What you put into it is what you get out of it." Succinctly and convincingly, she focuses on what you put in your mind and how those thoughts—positive or negative—manifest in life. An expert storyteller, Nancy shares Coco, a little cat, to remind us of our own humanity. A worthwhile read at any age.

Kelly Helmuth
Chief Growth Officer at Bestest, LLC

WHAT ARE YOU WAITING FOR?

WHAT ARE YOU WAITING FOR?
YOU DON'T HAVE 9 LIVES!

NANCY M. WEST

PUBLISH
YOUR
PURPOSE
PRESS

NANCY ⓜ WEST
B E C O M E ‖‖ M O R E

Publish Your Purpose Press
141 Weston Street, #155
Hartford, CT, 06141
www.PublishYourPurposePress.com

Ordering Information:
Quantity sales and special discounts are available on quantity purchases by corporations, associations, and others. For details, contact the publisher at the address above.

Printed in the United States of America.

Edited by: Heather B. Habelka
Cover design by: Owais Zaman
Cover photo by: Kimmo Virtanen (C) "Paws"
In creating the book cover, I wanted to capture the energy and essence of Coco and was blessed to find the photo of Alma, the little inquisitive kitty from Finland, who gave her human daddy the same type of love and joy as Coco shared with me.

ISBN: 978-1-946384-02-7 (paperback)
ISBN: 978-1-946384-43-0 (hardcover)
Library of Congress Control Number: 2017937185
First edition, June 2017, ii March 2018

Publish Your Purpose Press works with authors, and aspiring authors, who have a story to tell and a brand to build. Do you have a book idea you would like us to consider publishing? For more information please visit www.PublishYourPurposePress.com.

I will forever be in awe that I was graced for 16 years with an incredible bundle of love, fascination, and joy. To my little Coco, how I love you still.

ACKNOWLEDGEMENTS

There are so many people who have influenced me with their wisdom, love, and patience, who have always believed in me and who have helped me become the person I am today. In particular, I must thank my wonderful parents, and especially "Little Mom" for being my biggest cheerleader and listening to my endless ideas and nonsense, always encouraging me that I can do anything. To my crazy girlfriends Brynn and Sue for years of laughter, drying my tears, and holding me together when I failed miserably at something that I now look back on as a life event. To my dear friends John and Frances, who have opened my mind to the possibilities of being my best self. To Laura for helping me relish the freedom of believing in my self-worth and staying true to my heart. To Ann McIndoo, my Author's Coach, who initially got this book out of my head and into my hands. To my amazing writing and editing coach, Kelly Malone, for helping me polish the raw messages into a finished product. And finally, to Jenn T. Grace and her team at Publish Your Purpose Press, whose tenacity, expertise and humor kept me off the ledge and helped me make this book a reality. Each of you holds a very special place in my heart, and I am most grateful that you are all in my life. Little Coco would agree… trust me she would be hissing otherwise!

PREFACE

FOR MANY YEARS now I have wanted to create a series of workshops to help recent graduates work and live with greater fulfillment. That sounds so cliché, right? I thought I might build my series of workshops around a book, but I did not know where to begin, so I asked the Universe and listened to the whispers that were prompting me to move forward, not knowing how the output would manifest.

And then came Coco.

The snarky and sneaky little bundle whose intuition and brilliance urged me to start with *her story*: how she dealt with the situations in which she found herself, and how those situations related to the humans around her.

Coco's story is a quick, endearing read filled with thought-provoking messages, an exploration of the self-limiting behaviors of which we're all guilty, and ideas for how to reframe those behaviors while grounded in the essence of our authenticity. What makes us different, makes us special! Celebrating our unique abilities to create a zest for life can catapult growth individually, in our future profession after college, and in life.

Coco also wanted to clarify that I am not, by definition, a "crazy cat lady," in case you were wondering. Well, maybe I'm just a little twisted…

TABLE OF CONTENTS

THE PROFESSOR

IT WAS A beautiful spring afternoon and the professor waited in the green room until it was time for him to address the graduates. As he listened to the media mogul who was currently on stage, his thoughts wandered back to the conversation he'd had with a former student two weeks prior. During his thirty years in the public eye, he'd given hundreds of speeches, nationally and around the globe, often delivering his talks in languages other than his own native English. In other words, he had encountered more opinions than anyone would ever need. But it was his student's words that unsettled him, that had really thrown him for a loop. And now, here he was, about to address the graduating class of a Midwestern Big Ten University filled with students who were ready to embark on the next chapter of their lives and enter the workforce. Their majors and interests ranged from business, communications, criminal justice, education and medicine, just like thousands of graduates every year.

"What can possibly help them realize their full potential versus languish in making poor decisions based on prior beliefs that were embedded deep in their minds?" he asked himself. For the first time in his life, he was nervous about speaking.

All that got him to where he was—advanced degrees from Ivy League schools, stellar credentials, experience building and selling hugely successful businesses, best-selling books, lecturing, and now teaching—didn't seem to matter at this moment. He was as nervous as he could ever remember being. During the past thirty years, the professor had made hundreds of millions of dollars, giving much of it to causes he believed in. Being the humanitarian he was, he had always taken seriously the content of the many, many keynote speeches he'd given over the years (although he had to acknowledge his own fallback on clichés), but for this talk, he felt his message had to be different. He needed to give these graduates the tools that they didn't learn in college. Yes! He needed to share the tools and methods that took him years to understand and apply – that focusing internal thoughts on goals has the power to produce tangible results. How different their outcome could be if they apply today what took him years to understand?

As he listened to the current speaker, the professor thought, *It's the same old, same old.* That hollow rhetoric from seasoned veterans who told you to work hard to get ahead at all expense… blah, blah, blah. They never addressed the importance of listening to your inner thoughts and focusing on your true passion versus perhaps what your parents or coach or teacher told you to focus on. They never talked about how ignoring that passion and believing the negative words that once defined our actions can eat away at our ability to believe in who we are, which ultimately leads to a diminishing self-esteem. They spewed the same inauthentic metaphors he himself had spouted in his speeches over the years, and he knew these speakers were missing a key element of what it took to be successful in the workforce and in life. These graduates needed to hear more than his traditional commencement address.

His heart sank when he thought of giving the speech he'd cobbled together from previous boring, canned speeches—a speech no different from those he'd been listening to for the past sixty minutes. Again, he went back to the conversation with his student, to the story she had shared with him. He needed to share such insight with these graduates. He knew it now. He couldn't give the speech he had prepared. The students deserved more.

He looked at his watch and saw that it was time for him to head backstage. He stood up, dropped his notes in the trash, opened the door, and walked up the stairs. Backstage the production crew, sound engineers, and university staff ran back and forth, papers in hand, ripping off non-working headsets and calling for new ones, muttering and griping—in a frenzy to get ready for his speech. The professor sighed, "Classic lack of communication, typical backstage chaos," he said to himself.

A man in jeans and a green t-shirt yelled into his headset, "Grab the mic!" From where he stood, the professor could see the control booth at the back of the auditorium. In the booth, a man jumped up from his stool, waved his hands in frustration, then turned and yelled at someone in a baseball cap, who ran out of the booth and up to the stage with a mic. A man who the professor recognized as the producer, having checked with him earlier, grabbed the arm of a woman walking by, "Where the hell is his power pack? What are you waiting for, damn it? Get him wired, and make it quick!" The woman nodded, grabbed the audio equipment from the man in the green t-shirt, and, visibly drooping, hooked the professor's mic to his tie.

The professor had witnessed this scene before. Whether it was managers or teachers or coaches cutting down others to their core—like this producer, yelling, using words like "incompetent" and "stupid," spewing blame. The crew, in response, becoming more disengaged, losing what little respect they had for their boss, and then, of course, losing respect for themselves as they worked under such fierce scrutiny. This is what happens in the workforce, the professor thought, ALL the time—words that cut down people, nonconstructive criticism that impacts self-esteem, words that employees actually start to believe about their self-worth that can take a lifetime to erase! And in this case, the producer will wonder why his employees were so disengaged with such an important commencement event taking place. Were they unable to perform their job? Or were they unwilling to help each other because all they could focus on was how much they disliked their work environment and more specifically, their boss?

The man in the control booth worked the sound console, clearly trying to make sure that the volumes were in perfect balance. The producer muttered under his breath, "You idiot! You should've had this done hours ago! What is wrong with you people?" The professor could see the man in the control booth freaking out, the people backstage cowering in fear—all unhappy and resentful.

All at once, watching this demoralizing scene, a light bulb went off, and the professor realized he was no different from the producer. The professor had attributed his employees' poor performance—lack of clarity, inability to articulate where they saw themselves in three to five years, fear of speaking out if something wasn't right—to incompetence and lack of motivation. At that moment, he realized he had played a huge part in creating that behavior with his own employees.

The producer, seeing the professor staring and knowing the professor's reputation, started apologizing. "I'm sure you've seen this before. I'm sorry that they are so incompetent—I can't seem to hire the right people to do their jobs. You know how it is, you just can't find good people who actually want to work these days."

The professor barely smiled and proceeded toward the curtain.

On the stage, the emcee rattled off the professor's impressive credentials and his countless awards. From where he waited in the wings, the professor scanned the audience—eager, expectant, intense. Many of the graduates were ready to take notes and had various recording devices to capture his every word. He stood transfixed until someone nudged him and, to deafening applause, he stepped onstage, striding toward the center light.

Gripping the podium, the professor stared out at the audience. Usually, by now, adrenaline would be pumping through his system, and passion would fuel his perfect sentences, delivered with just the right combination of fire and gravity. But at that moment, he felt vulnerable, nervous and unsure. Some of the people in the audience looked behind him, and he turned and spotted a PowerPoint slide blown up on the screen, his name and the University's logo splashed across the projection area. The professor searched the room and found the control booth where the producer now stood. "I won't be needing those PowerPoint slides," he said. "Please turn off the projector."

The producer shook his head and said something the professor couldn't hear. Even from the podium, the professor could see he was livid. Not one for last-minute changes, the professor thought. Tightly wound was an understatement. He turned his focus to the audience—undergraduates ready and eager to listen to what will be their last group event as classmates before they enter the next phase in their lives. If he didn't say something to shake them up, they could very well enter the workforce with all the aspirations in the world only to find themselves knocked to their core just like the producer's crew.

"I want you all to listen," the professor said. "I want to share a message with you about becoming successful in life, a message that has nothing to do with anything you have learned throughout all the years you've spent here."

In the background, the professor could see the producer behind the glass booth in the back of the room, his hands flailing, assistants scurrying about the room. He knew he was causing confusion, doing something different than what was expected, but he also knew it was the right thing to do.

"Over the years," the professor said, "I've spoken in front of groups of people from 50 to 3,000, and these speeches have always been the same. Today is going to be different. In fact, I've thrown out my notes and shut down my PowerPoint presentation. I'm flying blind, and that's good, because I feel compelled to share something different with all of you about what it takes to find success in your life, in your workplace, and in the world. Today I'd like to share a story that was told to me very recently by one of my favorite students. Not many years ago, she was sitting right where you are now."

The professor grabbed a tall director's chair, pulled it toward the middle of the stage, and sat down. A single spotlight shone on him. Other than an occasional sneeze, the audience was silent, the air still, and an incredible, almost palpable pulse of energy was evident. The graduates seemed to lean in to this energy, alert and listening. After what seemed to be an eternal pause, someone from the back of the audience politely shouted, "What are you waiting for?"

The professor looked toward where the question had come

from. "What are you waiting for? Hmm. Good question. In fact, that's exactly what we are going to talk about today."

"A few weeks ago, I ran into a former student at Starbucks. She had taken several of my classes at least seven or eight years ago. At first, I didn't recognize her. She was no longer a student in jeans and a t-shirt with circles under her eyes from too little sleep and too much studying. She is now very professional, very put together. I was impressed. And yet, even though time had passed, she still had that special sparkle in her eye. She immediately came up to me and gave me a hug. 'Professor,' she said, 'It's so good to see you after all these years.'"

"To be perfectly honest, I was a little uncomfortable, because I couldn't recall her first name! But I did remember she was a very bright student, always inquisitive and eager to learn. Thank goodness Starbucks prints each customer's name on the side of the cup. After what I hoped was a surreptitious glance at her coffee, I got her name, and relaxed into what I thought would be a casual conversation with a former student. How wrong I was!"

"How are things going for you?" I asked her. "I'd love to hear what you've been up to."

"Well, a lot has changed since I've last seen you," she said. "I feel much wiser now."

I totally missed her comment about being wiser, and I immediately started talking about myself. When I finally figured out that I was being a lousy listener, I felt my face flush and I backtracked, blurting out, "You feel wiser now? Well, I hope I can take some credit for that." We both laughed.

Then my former student said, "What I learned in your classes was only part of it. I've learned a life lesson that can't be taught in the classroom."

I wasn't used to being challenged. Nobody stood up to me that way. And yet here she was, not a colleague or a rival, but a former student, doing just that. Feeling I'd been taken down a peg and yet curious, I looked at her and said, "Well, you didn't face death, did you? You still look alive and well to me."

"Yes," she said. "I did face death, and not very long ago."

Of course, I immediately felt horrible. "I'm so sorry," I said. "Please forgive me for being insensitive."

The professor looked out to the graduates. "You can imagine how terrible I felt," he said.

"You said you had faced death," I said to her. "If it's not too personal, I would like to hear about it."

"Well, I could share it," she said, "but I'm afraid you might think I'm crazy."

"No, please," I told her. "I really do want to hear it. I'm willing to listen if you'd like to share."

"I may sound a little *woo-woo*, but what I'm about to tell you profoundly changed my life," she looked past my shoulder, remembering. "It all started with the death of someone very, very special in my life. During the hours that preceded her death, it was as though her entire life flashed before my eyes as well as hers, and we had the most amazing connection that still leaves me trembling."

I felt my throat close just a little bit, and took a gulp of my coffee. I knew this was going to be difficult to hear, but I sure wasn't going to miss it.

"On her last day," she said, "as I held her, she let me know, in her own way, that people should not wait to follow their passion. We need to teach others how to harness the power of manifestation because it can accelerate our true potential and let us create the ideal life we visualize living. I promised her that when the time was right, I would share our story. As risky as it is, today feels like the right time."

The professor took a sip of water from the bottle on the podium and slowly began with his former student's story, in nearly a whisper.

"She was brave," he said. "She was amazing, and she faced death nine times."

CHAPTER ONE

NINE LIVES—LIMITLESS

THE HUMANS WERE at it again. Drumming their fingertips on the glass walls of Coco's room in the shelter, rapping their knuckles to get her attention. She tried to go back to sleep, curling up into a tiny black-and-white ball of fur. She was a tiny kitten, barely five weeks old. She was growing. She needed her rest. The drumming continued. "Look at the adorable tuxedo kittens." Coco poked her head up and opened one bright blue eye. A woman with spiked red hair smiled through the glass. "Hellooooo," she said. "Kittykittykitty."

Coco tilted her head to one side. *Are you trying to get MY attention?* She was the runt, with a curly-bent tail that her brothers and sisters called *deformed*, but she secretly considered it unique. Even if the woman was trying to get her attention, did Coco want to go home with her? She didn't think so. The woman made her skin itch.

She tapped again. Pink fingernails striking the smudged glass. *Could you stop tapping? Maybe stop staring and just make up your mind?* It was exhausting to be on display, to have people peering into her home, disturbing her sleep. Every day people knocked on the glass, and—because Coco didn't know anything about them, and certainly wasn't ready to change homes yet again—she tried to hide in the mound of fur that was her brothers and sisters, lying very still, tail down, curling up as tight as she could.

The woman kept peering at her. Coco ignored her; she had made up her mind that she definitely did not want to go with this woman. Coco heard a bark from the room next door and looked over. A man in a t-shirt was picking up the little yellow puppy and taking him out of his glass room. Another D.O.G. adopted. *Why did so many people love those smelly droolers?* One by one they left the shelter, only to be replaced by another and another. Were her brothers and sisters going to be adopted before her—one by one—leaving her with one less sibling, until she was the last left in the shelter? And only because, at five weeks, she was the smallest?

Taptaptap. *Seriously?* Coco put her head down, closed her eyes to a slit, peeking out from under her paw. She saw the woman turn away and hurry off. Was she really leaving? *Yes. Gone! Phew.*

"Hello little one." Coco turned, ears perking up. A woman with a black-and-white, fuzzy sweater pressed her nose against the window. Her outfit looked a little like Coco's mother's, but this was a human, not a cat. She looked straight at Coco. "Look how cute you are!" she said. "So tiny."

She didn't tap on the window with her fingernails; she just talked directly to Coco. She couldn't believe it. The woman's eyes were so kind and she had such a sweet voice. Coco felt entranced.

Maybe, just maybe, *this* woman might adopt her? Suddenly, Coco was ready to take the plunge, to leave her glassed-in home. More than anything in the world, Coco wanted to go home with this woman. This was her new mama. She knew it.

But then, wait! The red-haired woman was coming back, pulling the shelter manager by her shirtsleeve, pointing into the room, urging her to hurry as she unlocked the glass window. The minute it was open, the red-haired woman stuck her hand in, reaching for Coco—fingers splayed, sharp ring threatening, fingers coming closer, closer, closer.

"Hey," yelled the woman in the black-and-white sweater.

Red Hair ignored her.

Coco opened her mouth wide, showed her tiny sharp teeth, and growled, fierce, the mini roar she had perfected to keep her brothers and sisters from teasing her. This was not the right mama.

"I saw her first," her new maybe-mama yelled.

Wow! Coco thought. First, she had been worried that no one would want her, and now two people were fighting over her. Waving her curly-bent tail, she looked around the room, amazed. She was going first! She wouldn't have to watch her siblings leave her, one by one. She had spent so much time worrying about whom she'd end up with, that she had not for a second considered she would find the perfect new mama! It was crazy to think that already she couldn't imagine living with anyone else. Coco was so excited, she couldn't stop her tail from waving—thump to the right, hitting the floor, tiny pieces of confetti paper flying into the air. Thump to the left.

Her possible mama watched, in love. "Look at your adorable tail!"

Red Hair drew back her hand. "Okay, okay," she said, reaching for one of Coco's brothers. "They're all the same. They're all cute."

True, Coco thought. *We ARE all cute, but we are NOT all the same. Isn't it obvious?* Her new mama reached for her, and lifted her out. "Oh," Mama said, "You're absolutely the cutest of them all." The way she said it, with such conviction, Coco believed her.

"Look at you. So fuzzy." Mama held Coco against her heart and nuzzled her, then scratched her gently behind her ears. Coco purred. She could get used to this new heartbeat, and she knew that, unlike her cat mama, whose heartbeat she still missed, this woman wasn't going anywhere. As her new mama headed toward the door, Coco peeked over her shoulder at her brothers and sisters. Would she ever see them again? For a minute, even though she mostly felt safe with her new mama, she felt frightened and alone.

🐾 🐾

During the ride home, Coco huddled in the corner of her cardboard carrier, shaken, her eyes closed tight against the green dashboard light shining through the circles in the box. It was dark when they arrived at Coco's new home. Mama parked, walked around to Coco's side, and lifted the box, holding it steady, so Coco wouldn't slide from one side to the other. She entered the condo, walked down a hall, and set the box down outside what she called the second bathroom.

"Be right back," Mama said.

After a few minutes, Coco heard a rustling outside her box. She peered out the holes, and saw Mama placing what looked like huge pieces of confetti on the floor.

"Just putting down newspapers," Mama said, standing. "Hold on." She returned carrying a bag of kitty litter, a new litter box, a Mickey Mouse blanket that she called "Mickey blankie," a round fuzzy ball, a bag of kitty food, and a double pink bowl for water and food.

Cool water, crunchy food. Thirsty and starving, Coco meowed for her new mama to fill the bowls.

"Oh, poor thing," Mama said. "You must be starving." She dropped everything on the floor, picked up the double bowl, and filled one bowl with crunchies and the other with water. Coco was shivering, frightened, so Mama set the double bowl in her carrier box and continued to set up the room. Coco approached the bowl slowly, wary, then her hunger and thirst got the best of her, and losing all reserve, she lapped the water with her tiny tongue and crunched her way through her food.

When Coco finished her meal, Mama reached into the box, and gently lifted her out. Still frightened by her new surroundings, Coco sprang from Mama's arms, landed on the papers, and raced on wobbly legs to the back of the toilet, where she sat, safe between the toilet and the wall, peeking out from her hideout.

Mama stood, hands on hips, chewing her bottom lip. She looked from Coco to the litter box and back to Coco. Grabbing the litter box, Mama left the room, muttering something about Coco being too little for the litter box. She came back with a much smaller container. "It's the lid from a shoe box," she said, setting it down, ripping open the kitty litter, and filling the lid. "This is more your size. Do you need to go potty?"

Coco looked for the confetti that had lined her glass house at the shelter. Nothing. This was different. Then Mama picked her up, set her down in the shoe box lid, took her paw gently, and rubbed it several times in the kitty litter. *Oh, ok, I get it,* Coco thought, and she proceeded to do her business, looking up at Mama when finished. "That's right," Mama said. "You learn fast!"

Mama set Coco down. Sitting back on her haunches, Coco

looked up at her. "I hate to leave you alone," Mama said. "It's just for tonight. Until you get acclimated." She looked worried for a minute, her brow furrowing, then she smiled. "Wait here, little one."

She returned, carrying a big fuzzy animal with a black nose and round ears. "Here's a teddy bear to keep you company," Mama said, leaning the bear against the wall next to the toilet. "You can snuggle with the bear." Coco had no idea what a "bear" was, and the animal was eerily quiet, but at least she wasn't alone.

Sighing, Mama sat down on the paper and leaned against the cabinet. "You're so tiny," she said, her voice soft. "I could put you in the pocket of one of my t-shirts."

Oh, no. Is Mama going to start making fun of my size?

"That's what caught me," Mama said.

Maybe not. Coco sat on her back legs, her head tilted, eyes wide, almost as though she was going to spring.

"And your tail," Mama said. "The cutest tail ever."

It is pretty cute, Coco thought, thumping the newspaper.

"You're my first pet ever, you know," She smiled at Coco, amazed. "I'm a fast learner too, so don't worry. It's just for tonight."

Oh, she'd worry. For a while. How could she not? A new house? A new mother? But Mama seemed to want to learn, so excited and somewhat cautious, Coco thought she'd give her a chance.

The next day, when Mama opened the bathroom door, Coco was sitting on the floor, her little head tilted deep in thought. *What if Mama has buyer's remorse? The volunteer said she could return me if she changes her mind.* And as if Mama were clairvoyant, she said, "I have to confess, little one, I was happy when the shelter gave me a

100% return guarantee if we didn't work out, but one look at you, and I've fallen in love with you all over again."

From then on, when Mama was at home, Coco roamed the condo freely. On Mama's work days, Coco stayed in the second bedroom with her food, shoe box lid, and toys. Mama kept the door open, but she blocked the doorway with a piece of cardboard, just high enough so Coco couldn't jump over it. Not that she didn't try. She'd eye the height of the jump, leap, smash into the wall, slide down to the carpet, roll over, get back up, and try again. And again.

Some mornings, while Mama was getting ready for work and Coco was leaping and crashing and sliding, she could hear Mama laughing. She loved Mama's laugh. Wanting to be with her, Coco would double her efforts to escape. When that failed, she'd stand by the barricade and meow and meow. When Mama was at work, and Coco wasn't busy eating, sleeping, or playing with her toys, she'd start in again, attempting to jump the wall.

On the eighth day, Coco heard Mama in the kitchen making that hot black water that she drinks. That morning, she finally cleared the barricade. Free at last, she set out to find Mama. Coco strolled into the kitchen, nonchalant, as though she had all the time in the world, playing it down, as if Mama wouldn't notice. When she spotted Coco, Mama laughed and laughed. After that, Mama gave her free rein of the condo.

🐾 🐾

At first, Coco missed her brothers and sisters. She thought often of her cat mama. But she knew her new mama was here to stay. Mama played with Coco all the time, unlike her brothers and sisters, who ignored her. She missed Mama when she was at work, but she had her own work to do—lots of games to play and places to explore. And when she wasn't playing or exploring, she would curl up in a sunbeam, close her eyes, and listen to the sweet music of the birds outside.

Every morning after her breakfast, Coco dug around in her toy box, trying to decide which game to play first. Tease the stuffed mice? Chase the jingly light-up ball around the room? Drag the toy shoe-laces? Sometimes Coco liked to use her imagination and make her own toys. She could make toys out of anything! Everything had possibilities. Even the ritual called "opening presents" left so much colorful shiny paper to roll around in. And all those ribbons and bows! She loved stick-on bows, especially after she'd chewed on one, unraveling the bow into a long, crumply piece of ribbon. Such artwork!

Coco's favorite toy was a Q-tip. Fuzzy on both ends, flexible, and if she hit it just right with her paw, it would fly clear across the room. Of course it often went too far underneath Mama's bedroom door, where she couldn't get it. And if she tried—lying on her side, stretching her paw under the door, stretching even more—and Mama was in her room, she'd cackle, grabbing Coco's paw, squealing. Coco would play along for a while, but what she really wanted was for Mama to open the darn door, so she could get her toy.

Her second favorite toy was a crunched-up wad of paper. Actually, there was a whole pile of them in the circular can that seemed to get emptied once a week but was mysteriously and routinely refilled the following week, some ritual Mama called "paying bills." When Mama wasn't looking, Coco would put her two front paws on the edge of the can, and with all her weight, she would lean to knock it over, and *shazam! Paper balls! All different kinds of paper balls!*

Coco chewed on those paper balls and batted them with her paws. One day, when Mama was at work, and her paper ball went flying behind the couch, Coco maneuvered between the wall and the piece of furniture—not easy—to get it out. She had crawled behind the couch before, with no problem, but this time, as she was creeping toward the paper ball, something grabbed her. Coco pulled. *Ow! It hurts like crazy!* Just like when her brothers and sisters used to bite and paw her tail. She had thought that they were trying to hurt her, but when she confronted them, she found out they were truly trying to help straighten her tail that was curled twice and resembled a paperclip. "*That's how my tail is supposed to be,*" she meowed to her siblings, "*not straight like all of yours.*"

But she was not in the shelter, and her brothers and sisters weren't here. She had no idea what gripped her tail.

Coco heard the key in the front door, and then Mama calling "Coco. Hey, little one."

"Meow," Coco wailed.

"Coco?" Mama sounded worried. "Where are you?"

"Meoow. Meooow." Coco was scared and sad. And trapped. "Meoooow."

Mama dropped her briefcase and keys on the floor, and hurried to the couch. She pulled the couch from the wall, and crawled behind it. "Oh, Coco. Poor baby. Your tail's caught on the light cord." Gently, gently, Mama untangled her tail, and Coco sprang free, then waited, wanting Mama to comfort her.

After that, Coco didn't want to play. Mama went into the kitchen, returned with a treat, and sat on the floor next to Coco, who climbed on her lap. "Coco," Mama said, "You scared me. When I heard you crying, I thought you'd just used up one of your nine lives." *What does that mean? If something really scary happens, I lose a life?*

I'd better be extra careful from now on, Coco thought, and for the next few days, she played only safe games, steering clear of the couch. Mostly, she played with Mr. Mousie. Coco loved the paper balls, but no way was she going behind the couch again. But by Saturday, Coco was bored to tears with Mr. Mousie and decided to pluck up her courage to play with the balls of paper. If a ball went under the couch, she decided, she would just leave it there.

Mama was in the kitchen, filling Coco's water and making lemonade, so the coast was clear for Coco to knock over the circular can and play. She tipped it over just as the doorbell rang.

Mama hurried in through the living room to answer the door. Coco froze. She wouldn't move; she'd just blend in with the paper balls. She was nervous about people coming in to her safe house.

"Hi, Ted," Mama said. "I'm so glad you could stop by." She stood aside as Ted walked in.

"Coco," Mama called. "Come meet our neighbor, my friend Ted."

Coco hunched down, peering at Ted above her stack of paper balls. *I don't think so,* she thought. *Who IS this guy? And what's up with his hair? Even I have better grooming habits!*

Ted's hair was matted as though he wore a hat all day. Faded jeans rode low on his hips. He had on a green hoodie and a black t-shirt bearing the logo of a now-defunct '80s rock band.

Mama smiled slightly when she saw Coco playing the "mannequin challenge" amidst all the paper balls that she knocked out of the trash, glaring at their visitor. "He helps with odd jobs around the condo complex. Fixes things," she said.

I hope he does a better job fixing things around the condo than he did fixing those glasses of his. He had wound a small piece of tape around the hinge of his glasses to hold them together.

"Anything goes wrong," Mama went on, "he's right there to help."

What does that have to do with ME? If anything goes wrong in my world, YOU help.

"He's going to watch you when I have to go on business trips. You know, feed you, refresh your water, change your litter. Maybe he'll even play Mr. Mousie with you."

"Absolutely," Ted said.

Coco turned her head away, toward the couch. *Whatever.*

"She's adorable," Ted said to Mama. Slowly, he walked over to Coco. "Aren't you, kitty?"

Kitty? Coco peered at Ted through narrowed eyes. *Really? My name is Coco. Is this visit over yet?*

Ted sat down next to Coco. "You don't like being called 'kitty,' do you?" he asked. "I'll stick with Coco then."

Hmmm. Maybe he isn't so bad. He seems to understand me.

"Coco," he said. "Why are you hiding in the trash?"

Or maybe not. I'm not hiding in the trash, she thought. *I'm hiding with my toys.*

Ted nodded, as he tossed a crumpled piece of junk mail from one hand to the other. "This is the perfect ball, don't you think, Coco? Do you like to fetch?"

"Cats don't fetch," Mama said, then caught the gleam in Coco's eye. "Do you fetch?" she asked her.

Ted tossed the paper ball. "One way to find out."

Yep. I do. Coco jumped up and ran across the room, pouncing, snatching the paper ball up in her mouth, and trotting it back to Ted, dropping it by his worn out, lace-free topsiders. She watched closely as he picked it up. Her eyes wide, ears perked up, all senses on high alert.

Ted tossed the paper ball again, and Coco took off.

"She likes you," Mama said.

"Yeah, well, animals and I understand each other." He sat, holding the paper ball, lost in thought. Coco butted his hand with her head.

"Sorry, Coco." He lobbed the paper ball across the room. "I always dreamed of becoming a veterinarian."

Mama walked over to the couch, sat down, and leaned forward, elbows on her knees. "Why didn't you?"

"I don't know. My parents said there wasn't much of a future for vets. I was a bit of a goof-off in school. Didn't really stick to anything for long. I had a few professors who said I wouldn't amount to anything—some of my friends said the same thing. I guess I believed them. It was a dream. That's all."

Coco had dreams—of climbing trees, of climbing anything high off the ground. She lived nine floors up. *Maybe those dreams wouldn't come true?*

"Dreams can come true," Mama said. "We have to be clear on what we want, then take action."

Phew.

Ted traced his fingers down the length of Coco's spine. "Imagine what it would be like to be surrounded by animals all day. I'd *love* to go to work."

"Take a class or two," Mama said. "Check it out."

Yeah, take a class, Coco thought.

"I don't know," Ted said.

Coco dropped the paper ball next to Ted's hand. *Why not?* she thought. *Why couldn't you be a veterinarian? Why couldn't your dream come true? And why won't you take a class?*

"It's a bit late in life for me to change direction."

"Please," Mama rolled her eyes. "You're only 32-years-old."

Ted sighed.

"Maybe you could volunteer at a shelter," Mama said.

Yeah, that's a great idea. Coco rubbed against Ted's knee. *You could be around cats all day. Maybe I'll come with you. You just have to bring me home at the end of your shift.*

Ted sighed. "It seems such a long way off—the goal. What if I don't stick to it? Then everyone will be right—I won't amount to anything."

"You have to believe," Mama said. "And you have to hang out with those who nurture your dreams, not smash them. Even then, you're the one who has to hold on to your dream—and take action, every small step counts!"

Coco licked her paws. *I'm lucky to have this mama.* She batted the paper ball. *Darn! Behind the couch. Oh, why not?* She'd watch out for the cord, and go for it. Mama was here.

"All you need," Mama said, "is to allow your imagination to

create your ideal life. Then, to really connect your true love and passion, take small steps to make it happen."

Coco paused behind the couch. *What's my passion?* she wondered. It could be climbing. Or something else? Well, she had nine lives to figure it out. All the time in the world. Getting stuck behind the couch didn't cause Coco to lose one of her nine lives because Mama was there to help. The sky is the only limit! Coco was filled with dreams, inspiration and ideas!

BECOME MORE:

- Find your heart's desire, your passion, and hold onto it, follow it.

- In order to foster your passion, move towards what interests you versus something that does not. Seek purpose by asking yourself, "What problem or issue can I solve?" Or, "How do I want the world to be different?" That will lead you toward the wisdom of Gandhi, "Be the change you wish to see in the world."

CHAPTER TWO

EIGHT LIVES—FIXING NOTHING WRONG

ONE YEAR LATER, Coco woke up with a big plastic cone on her head. She opened her eyes and moved her head to lick low on her belly, where her skin felt odd. But when she turned her head, she couldn't even see her legs, much less lick her belly. Or her tail. *I can't see my body!! Where did I go? What is going on?*

Panicked, she pulled at the cone with her paws, her small pink pads slipping on the smooth plastic. She turned her head and tried to bite her way free, then she stuck out her tongue and tried to lick her way out. *Help!* Where was Mama? *But wait, if I'm not here, how will Mama see me? I have to get out of this thing!*

Footsteps. Coco held her breath. It was Mama. She would know that scent anywhere. She had seen Mama spray some nice smelling stuff from a bottle on her neck, right where Coco liked to nuzzle. Help was on the way—if Mama could just see her.

"Hey, little Coco."

Phew. Mama can see me!

Mama sat down on the carpet, and reached for Coco's paw. "You're awake," Mama said. "Your poor little body."

Okay, well that's good. My body's here. Coco sat up. She put her paw on Mama's knee, and started to climb onto her lap, but halfway there, she lost her balance, and rolled onto the floor. "Meow!" Coco slit her eyes and looked searchingly at Mama.

"Oh, Coco." Mama leaned over, scooped her up, and settled Coco on her lap. "I know. Don't worry, we'll take your cone off when the doctor removes your stitches."

Stitches? Coco peered at Mama.

"We had you fixed," Mama said.

Fixed? There was nothing wrong with me to have fixed in the first place. Was there? Is getting fixed becoming invisible? Is visibility bad?

"It's a weird term," Mama said, as though reading her mind. "The surgery is also called 'getting spayed.' It's to prevent you from having kittens, in case you ever get out." Mama scratched Coco behind her ears.

Does being able to have kittens mean you're broken? Coco was confused and curled up tighter. She would never have her own kittens. That was pretty sad. On the other hand, she was relieved she wouldn't have kittens to worry about or share with Mama. She liked her life here with Mama. Just the two of them. She liked things the way they were.

"You still have eight more lives," Mama whispered softly.

What? Only eight? Yesterday I had nine lives. What happened Mama?

"All cats are born with nine lives Coco, unlike people who only have one. With each major trauma or challenge you face, you lose a life," Mama said, "But you get to start a new one until you run out of time."

Really? How much time do we have Mama? Why didn't I get a say in this? It was all too much. Coco closed her eyes and drifted off to sleep.

🐾 🐾

Coco awoke to a knock on the door.

"That must be Ted." Mama stood up to let him in, setting Coco gently on the carpet, where she curled up, still groggy. "He called to say he wanted to check up on you."

As soon as Mama opened the door, Ted tiptoed in, hands behind his back. "How is she?" he whispered.

"She's awake," Mama said, "You don't have to whisper. You look awful, by the way."

"I know, but let's focus on Coco," he said, as he tiptoed to the couch, gently waving a stick with a stuffed bird dangling from it—orange with pink and purple wings. "Look, Coco!" He waved the stick again, almost reluctantly, as though not to excite her.

Rolling on her back, Coco turned her head to get a better look at the toy.

Ted held the stick above Coco's head, dangling the bird just out of reach. "Careful," he said.

Coco stood up and jumped, front legs extended to bat the bird, forgetting for a moment about the cone. But she couldn't see beyond the rim of her cone. Pawing the air, she fell flat on her stomach. This cone was so frustrating. She didn't even have a fighting chance.

Ted dangled the bird in front of her. "You can do it, Coco."

Coco meowed, swung. Nothing.

Mama and Ted exchanged looks.

What does THAT look mean? I'll never play bird on a stick again? Getting fixed ruined me? Angry, frustrated, Coco dropped her coned head to the floor. She was absolutely not going to play this game anymore.

"Oh, Coco," Mama said. "I'm so sorry. You'll be fine soon. I promise."

I'm not moving.

Ted sat back. "I know just how she feels." He laid the toy across his lap, shoved his hand through his sandy brown hair.

He must have washed it, Coco thought. *It usually looks matted down.*

Mama sank to the floor next to Ted and Coco. "What's going on, Ted?"

Hello? I'm the one with the cone around my neck. Not Ted.

"I had my mid-year review this week. I got criticized because I let a member of the team present MY ideas as their action plan for our client as if it were their own. I was afraid to speak up."

Poor Ted, but I'm not getting how this relates to ME.

"You need to be more assertive," my boss said. "Then he called me a 'bleeding heart' like it was the worst thing in the world. He said I was 'soft' and I lack confidence."

Still waiting for the connection… and speaking of bad weeks, can we discuss something besides hospitals and bleeding hearts? Maybe YOU need a cone too!

"I feel so defeated."

Aha, there we go. Get to the point Ted so you can focus on ME.

"Have you called St. Francis Animal Hospital and Rescue to volunteer?" Mama asked. "Working at the emergency hospital might cheer you up."

"I just can't face starting something new right now," Ted pushed his glasses up on his nose. "I guess what people have always said is true. I'm too sensitive and afraid of my own shadow."

"Words can hurt," Mama said. "Sometimes we hear words and believe them, especially when we hear them repeatedly. We can build whole stories around those beliefs. Take Coco."

Hey, wait a minute.

"She's having a hard time playing with her new toy, right? Well, what if I were to tell her she didn't know how to play with her toys and that she was just a dumb cat?"

Excuse me?

"She might believe it," Mama said. "She might stop playing. And she loves her toys—her mousie, her ribbon, her paper balls. Can you imagine how sad that would be? Can you imagine how that would change her life if she believed what other people told her as truths?"

I'd never believe people who said that. Then she thought about how sensitive she was about her little size and her unusual tail that was curled twice and resembled a paperclip. Coco then reflected on how some people would point to her at the shelter and say nobody would adopt a kitten with a deformed tail! *Didn't they know I could hear them?* It was very hurtful. *Like Ted, maybe I was just as afraid to speak up? I should have hissed!*

"You're right," Ted said.

"Also, those words that might seem negative in one environment might be just the opposite in another," Mama said. "Empathy and sensitivity are necessary qualities in a veterinarian."

Ted sighed, "I guess so."

"Call the hospital," Mama said.

Ted pushed himself off the floor, dropping the stick as he stood. He bent to retrieve it, stumbled slightly, and *snap!* The stick was in two pieces.

You broke my toy!

"Oh, no," Ted said. "I'm so sorry, Coco."

"Coco knows you didn't mean it." Mama smiled at Coco.

Coco narrowed her eyes. *I'm not so sure about that.*

"I have to go to the hardware store later," Ted said. "I'll pick up a stick. I can fix it."

That word again—fix. *Why had Mama used that word to describe the operation if the real word was 'spayed?'*

"Thanks, Ted," Mama opened the door. "Call St. Francis."

Mama shut the door, and then came over to Coco and knelt down. Coco looked at her and meowed. She was so lucky to have Mama. Mama would 'fix' her bird. Or would she 'spay' her bird?

When I got 'fixed' Mama said I was spayed. So if she fixes the bird, is it getting spayed? I'm so confused when two words can mean the same thing! Mama picked up each half of the stick. "Poor bird," she said.

Coco kept her head on the floor, resting in the cone. Mama took the bird and placed it on the carpet, near Coco's paws.

Coco looked at Mama. *What now?*

"We'll just toss out the stick," Mama said, freeing the bird and the string.

But it's broken. It's not the same. Coco felt heartbroken.

"And look." Mama held up the bird on the string. "A new lease on life. The bird is actually better while different."

Lying on her stomach, Mama set the bird right in front of Coco, where Coco could reach it.

Coco blinked her eyes, slowly. She didn't know if she liked this new bird, this broken bird.

"C'mon, Coco." Pulling the string, Mama made the bird dance and hop on the carpet, always in Coco's sight. "You just have to see the toy differently. The bird is okay, see?"

Before she could stop herself, Coco reached out and struck the bird. *Aha!*

Mama continued to play, helping Coco to catch the bird. "Oh, you little weasel," Mama said, "You're so adorable."

Coco lunged at the toy and Mama.

Mama laughed. "There's absolutely nothing wrong with you being different from all of your brothers and sisters."

"That's why I chose you. You were different. You were the tiniest little kitten of them all with a very curly tail that looked like a paperclip and that caught my attention—as well as my heart. Our differences make us special!"

Coco lunged at the bird, batted it, rolled on her back, and stared up at Mama.

Mama pulled it back. Too far. Coco turned her head away from Mama.

Mama laughed. "You are such a little diva."

What did Mama expect? With a name like Coco—short for Coco Chanel—she was destined to grow up like royalty. She looked up at Mama. Mama said her friends called her 'Queenie.' Coco had been adopted by a Queen! Mama always bought Coco treats, and gave her fresh water, and delicious food that the vet told her would help her grow and keep her fur glossy. Coco had started out in a shelter and ended up in a palace. Nine floors up on the Gold Coast. Why they called it *gold*, she had no idea. It wasn't. But someone in Cleveland had labeled it the Gold Coast, and the name had stuck. *Wow! Am I lucky.*

Mama had told her that doing what you like is freedom, and liking what you do is happiness. That was great advice. She had eight lives left. It was time to get started with the new one.

BECOME MORE:

- Words can carry an impact from those who speak them if we allow it, so what we do once we hear them is key. Don't let those words, opinions, judgments—or the people who speak them—define who you are.

- A great resource is *The Four Agreements*, by Don Miguel Ruiz. One of his concepts, when it comes to managing feedback from others, is to *not take anything personally.* Many times people say things to us because of their own limitations and beliefs, not yours. Think about that next time... it will help you put feedback into perspective!

CHAPTER THREE

SEVEN LIVES—EXPLORING
THE POSSIBILITIES

AS COCO GREW into a little cat, she dreamed more
and more of climbing trees—jumping from the
grass to the bottom limb, stretching her legs,
springing, flying, and scrambling up dry, gnarly
bark. She saw cats jumping up into trees on TV,
and somehow, deep inside her, she just knew
how it felt, remembered it in her very bones, the
freedom, the thrill. She loved to sit by the living
room window, gazing down from the ninth floor at the
tops of the trees below. She knew someday she'd get
down there, but in the meantime she needed to
practice. She had been climbing up on the coffee
table, the dining room table (when Mama wasn't
home), and the couch, practicing jumping off—
she was getting really good, but she longed to climb,
really climb.

One day, after Mama left for work, Coco sauntered into the

kitchen, the tile cool on her paws, sat back on her haunches, and scanned the room. She was tired of looking up. She needed a new perspective. Head back, she scoured the room, and spotted the perfect perch—the top of the cabinet.

She could see herself up there, pictured looking down on the sink and the counter, the floor. She'd rule the world! It was her right. When she first attempted to jump from the floor to the coffee table, the jump had seemed really high, almost impossible. But she tried and tried, and she finally made it! Then when she wanted to jump higher, from the floor to the back of the couch, she'd had to push harder, spring more. Again, it had taken practice and focus on her goal. So maybe that's what she needed to do now—push really, really hard. Really spring.

She sat, focusing and seeing herself on the top of the white cabinet. It was going to be tough, wedging into that eight-inch space between the cabinet and the ceiling. She planned to jump, and then propel herself in sideways. Midair. Or something.

Coco scrunched down on her back paws and jumped as high as she could go—eyes on the top of the cabinet—focused. And thud, she was back on the floor, rolling on her back, to her stomach, and back on all fours, focused on the cabinet the way she focused on a bird in a tree in her dreams. She focused, focused, sprung. And fell. She felt discouraged, but she kept at it. She couldn't get more than about a third of the way up to her goal. *I need a break.* She strode to her dish and lapped up some clean, cold water. Maybe she would just stay there. Forever. By the water bowl, right next to her food. That was a view she could live with—or was it?

For a minute, she let herself feel discouraged. Mama had said dreams could come true. She so wanted to be on top of the cabinet—higher than she ever thought possible. That was her goal. Coco could see herself up on the cabinet—her vision. What if she couldn't make it, though? What if she lacked what it took to make this dream a reality? *Enough meowing*, she thought, and sat down, head up, eyes on the top of the cabinet, looking, thinking.

Then she saw her first step. If she moved over to the sink area, she could jump up to the countertop. That would get her partially to her goal. She sat back, scrunched her legs and sprang! Bam! *I did it! I'm on the counter.* "MEOW!" Her heart pounded with excitement. *Almost there.* That cabinet didn't look so high now. *I can do this. I know I can do this!*

Savoring her victory, Coco toured the countertop, exploring all the things she had seen from the floor. It was a whole new world up here. *Everything looks different from this perspective!* She spotted the shiny thing with slots on top, where Mama put bread that popped back out. And darker! *Better not knock that around. Mama won't be able to make breakfast.* She saw the machine that made hot black water that smelled good. Mama would pour it into a cup and hold it between her hands, breathing in the smell, closing her eyes. *Better not jump on that either. Mama would be really upset.*

Okay, back to the cabinet. *What to do next?* Again, she scanned the room. Scanning, scanning. *Aha! The top of the refrigerator.* What if she jumped up there? She hoped it didn't have slots on top that she could fall into like that shiny bread thing. *That would be scary… or maybe it could be really fun. I vote for fun!* Coco thought, and decided to jump higher.

Concentrating with all her might, Coco scrunched down on her hind legs. *One, two, three—JUMP! Wheeee!* She was on top of the fridge! She looked down—aerial view of the counter, the floor, her bowl of crunchies. This was another different view, just higher. Now all that was left was only a short hop to the top of the cabinet. She could hunch down a little, and jump right up. Coco focused, eyes on the prize, jumped, and *Yes!* She had arrived!

She looked down, heart pounding. She was really, really high— right next to the ceiling. She'd never thought she could do that when she'd been on the floor. She'd have to figure out some way to celebrate her huge accomplishment. She had to somehow share her accomplishment with Ted. This one-jump-at-a-time, take action method could really help him reach his goals!

And then she thought about Mama. What would Mama think if she saw her up there? She thought about it and knew Mama would understand how exciting it was for Coco to be up high. Coco was just like her mama, who chose to live high off the ground on the ninth floor. Coco laid down and closed her eyes. She'd done it. And then she heard the key in the lock. Mama was home early. "Coco," called Mama. "Ted's coming over. We're going to give you your first mani pedi."

❧ ❧

An hour later, Ted left with his clippers, and Coco lay under the end table, back to Mama, who'd just closed the front door and was on her way over. *Don't even think about coming over here,* Coco thought. Mama had conspired with Ted, held Coco down while he (who had promise but whose only current qualifications were volunteer hours at PetSmart) clipped her nails shorter. *That awful sound!* 'Trimming' they'd called it. "Mani pedi," Mama had said. As though it was a good thing. *Ha! That was a barbaric surgery.* Even though there had been absolutely no blood and no pain, the possibility had been there.

Another traumatic experience—or was it? *In my mind, I was never so scared!* That meant she had lost another life. At least she had made good use of her past eighth life, but now she had seven lives left. But was that progress wasted? How could she ever climb again with her short claws?

"That wasn't so bad, was it?"

Coco turned her head, eyes slit. *Wasn't so bad? How about we hold YOU down and do the same!* Mama was crouching down, peering under the table. "Ted really seems to have a knack," Mama said.

A knack for cutting me down in my prime, Coco thought. *I'll probably never climb a tree. Never jump again. Period.* Had Mama been angry because she jumped so high? Is that why her nails had been 'trimmed?' Or did Mama, like her brothers and sisters, want her to just blend in? She wouldn't do it.

"Don't look so sad," Mama said. "By the way, did I tell you how amazing I think it is that you jumped to the top of the cabinet? Just like a mountain lion."

Coco closed her eyes. *It doesn't matter now*, she thought. *I can still jump, but can I ever climb a tree with these stumps for claws?* What if a big animal were chasing her? What if she got picked on? Her brothers and sisters had picked on her because she'd been the runt. What if? What if? What if? She had grown, but she was still tiny for being a year old. She wasn't in the clear yet. Mama called the people who picked on others "bullies." It wasn't fair. If it was so wrong, why did it happen? But anyway, why was she spending time worrying about being chased up a tree by an imaginary bully that was only in her mind? *Did I make this scarier just thinking about something negative that hasn't even come true? Meow…*

She guessed it was a good thing she was an indoor kitty, as

Mama explained. No big animals would ever hurt her as long as she lived in the high-rise palace. She was so safe with her mama. As long as she could jump to the top of the cabinet and find new places to survey her world, that was all that mattered. As long as she could think of new challenges. She didn't want to waste a minute more worrying. After all, she still had seven lives.

BECOME MORE:

- Regain your sense of wonder, what's important to you, and set high goals. Then get creative and take the first step. Take action.

- Act, and thank the Universe, as if what you want has already come to be. For example, say, "I am so grateful for finding the ideal job that has me working with little animals everyday, making a difference in their lives and the humans who they live with." Say this before it actually happens. This will help it manifest.

CHAPTER FOUR

SIX LIVES—ASSUMPTIONS AND AUTHENTICITY

A T TWO YEARS old, Coco's curly tail grew longer and really resembled a paperclip. One day, Coco had been chasing Mr. Mousie under the end table, when, deep in the game, she hooked her curly paperclip tail around the lamp cord she had always been so careful to avoid. Trapped, she'd howled for Mama, meowed as loud as she could, as close to a lion's roar as she could get, but Mama wasn't home. An hour later, when Mama unlocked the front door, she found Coco crying, trying to gnaw through the black rubbery wire to get free.

"Coco, stop!" Mama ran to the table. "You'll electrocute yourself!" Coco had no idea what "electrocute" meant, but Mama seemed to think it was terrible, so she stopped, and waited, shivering while Mama knelt down and freed the cord wrapped around her tail. "I can't bear the thought of losing you, Coco," Mama said. "I love you so much." Then Mama sat down on the couch with

Coco, holding her, shushing her, until Coco finally stopped shivering and fell asleep, safe.

After the cord incident, Mama met with a surgeon, who told her she could help Coco by docking her tail at the first hook. So now, two years after Mama had picked her out of the litter, partially because of her curly-bent tail, Coco had a new tail, a shorter tail. Almost no tail, really.

❧ ❧

Mama and Coco played on the floor, but Coco couldn't focus—she twisted and turned to get a peek of her tail over her shoulder.

"It's still there," Mama said. "It's just short. It's really cute."

Coco twisted, lost her balance, fell on her side, and stayed there, demoralized and sad she was down to six lives.

"It's moving," Mama said. "Just not nearly as much."

Right. How can it move? It's too short. Would people make fun of this tail too? Everyone had made such a big deal of her curly-bent tail, always asking Mama what had happened to her, what was wrong with it. How rude was that? "Nothing's WRONG," Mama always said. "That's her tail. I think it's great." Sometimes these questions hurt Coco's feelings, but sometimes they made her mad—then she'd get the last word in with a hiss. Conversation over.

Coco rolled over, flat on her stomach, front legs extended, and dropped her head between her front paws, face down on the carpet. *I've pretty much had it with being teased.*

"Coco," Mama said, "It's going to be okay. To hell with other people. Let's talk about 'acceptance.' In the world, people have all kinds of things that make them special. In your case, you have a tiny tail*, and that's just one* of your many unique qualities. I love you just the way you are. People don't have tails, little one, but they do have physical differences. Some people are tall, others are short, some are large, some small; this is what makes each person interesting. You know what the real Coco Chanel said? 'In order to be irreplaceable, one must always be different.' Think about that, weasel."

❖ ❖

A few days later, Ted came to check on Coco. He dropped on his knees in front of where she lay by the couch and started tickling her stomach. "How are you, Coco?"

"She's doing better," Mama said, as she sat down on the couch.

Hellooo. I'm right here. I can answer.

Mama turned to Ted. "How are *you*?"

Really? That's all the airtime I get?

Ted took a deep breath. "I went to St. Francis Animal Hospital and Rescue to see about volunteering."

"That's great!"

Mama suggested that two years ago when I was a baby! Why did it take so long if this is your dream job? What are you waiting for?

Ted held his hands up. "They have no volunteer positions. They're all internships! You need to be registered in school to get one."

Mama leaned forward. "You'll just have to sign up for a class then."

That's it, Ted. Problem solved. So back to how I'm feeling… a little odd, sore—

"I did," Ted said. "I even looked into a few graduate programs, but since my B.A. is in communications, I need fifteen more credits in science to apply. So I signed up for marine biology at Cuyahoga Community College for next quarter."

Fish? What is he thinking? How to catch big ones to feed me?

"I went to register. I'm ten years older than everyone else. I feel so old, like an entirely different species."

Hey, I'm with you on that one. Look at this tail! This is not the tail of a cat. I only have a stump to wag.

"Look at Coco," Mama said.

That's what I just said.

"Sure, her tail is little now. It's as cute as it was before. Just different. And now she can play without getting stuck."

Then again. Coco stood up, stretched, and pranced around. *Revel in your difference.*

"Younger students—their brains are more nimble," Ted said. "I'm out of practice. I've forgotten everything that's still fresh in their minds. They can stay up all night cramming. Those days are gone for me."

Better switch those thoughts around, Ted, Coco thought. *Positive thoughts! Mama's drilled that into my head.*

"Seriously, Ted?" Mama slapped him playfully on the arm. "You use your brain every day at work."

Ted sighed. "My boss would argue the opposite." He leaned to the side before Mama could slap him again.

And you believe your boss? Why not believe what YOU know about yourself?

Mama slapped her fist in her palm. "If you keep thinking you can't, those thoughts will just keep running through your mind, over and over, until you believe them."

"Work doesn't help."

Mama sighed, "I love you, Ted, but I swear, sometimes, it's like pushing a rock uphill with you. You're probably in the wrong job. The wrong career. You can't change who you are to fit in. It's a terrible idea."

Coco stopped strutting and blinked at Ted. *You've got to be authentic. It's what Mama always tells me. Be the best Coco you can be!*

"You've got to turn those limiting thoughts around."

"That sounds like too much work," Ted said.

"Only at first. But in the long run, it's less work, because your life will get easier. It's like wearing a cone around your neck like Coco's had to do."

Oh, no way, Coco thought.

"Wearing a cone can restrict your vision, narrow your focus," Mama said. "You can't see your way out."

Amen, Coco thought.

"On the other hand—"

Here we go. Mama was on a roll. Why is Mama obsessing about cones? I'm so over cones.

"Cones can be good, theoretically. Placing a cone around your mind can help you keep your dreams alive or rediscover old ones you may have buried. Focus on positive words," Mama said, "and positive thoughts to create what you want."

Wait, Coco thought. *While people change their thoughts, do they have to wear a cone around their heads? Not gonna happen.*

"Not a real cone," Mama said, reading Coco's mind. "It's a metaphor. Focus. Think positive. Take action. Maybe put in five minutes more of practice each day. Thoughts plus action equal change. See yourself having the best day, best week, best year of your life."

Ted relaxed his shoulders. "Thank you," he said to Mama. He reached over and scratched Coco behind her ears. "And thank you, Coco. I came over to see how you are, and I only talked about myself. Thanks for sharing your mama."

Coco purred. She was lucky to have Ted. And they were both so lucky to have Mama.

🐾 🐾

Coco had loved her curly-bent tail. Because of that tail, she learned to appreciate differences. She learned to stand tough with her brothers and sisters, meowing with the ferocity of a lion—wild, hunched back, ready to spring. She learned to analyze situations, to strategize when playing, to avoid tangling herself in cords (successful for the most part). She had developed skills to steer clear of pitfalls, to slink past, wind around, slide under.

As the days went by, Coco learned to love her new shortened little tail. She had such freedom now. She wasn't afraid of people making fun of her tail. After a few weeks, Coco decided to show Mama her new skills. When Mama came home that night, set down her briefcase and called for Coco, Coco decided it was time to show her stuff.

I'm here. Coco meowed from the far end of the living room. Then, with Mama watching, Coco took off, speeding toward the couch, zipping through the narrow space between the couch and the wall, past the cords, and out the other side, under the end table, speeding on, flipping from too much excitement, head over heels, landing in a belly flop by Mama's feet. Mama laughed so hard she couldn't stop, and Coco laid there, legs splayed, happy. She loved this new life, but only after she accepted change that actually made her more nimble and fast and feeling very proud for once about her special tail.

BECOME MORE:

- Fear blankets our authentic talents, purpose, and beliefs. Accepting change and acknowledging the gifts it can bring is a powerful new beginning.

- A tool to help deal with self-limiting beliefs whenever they arise is to ask yourself, "Says who?"

    For example, "I'm not experienced enough to apply for this position."

    Says who?

    Do companies find every single item listed on a job description within one college graduate applying for the job? Or do they hire the person that has the best positive attitude and then teach them the work where they can gain the experience? Think about that!

CHAPTER FIVE

FIVE LIVES—THOUGHTS BECOME THINGS

AT FIVE YEARS old, Coco grew into a majestic little tuxedo cat. One day, she sat on the windowsill, soaking up sun, waiting for Mama to get home from her business trip. Mama was a sales representative covering seven states and went out of town nearly every week from either Monday through Thursday or Tuesday through Friday. When Mama was gone, Ted stopped by after work to take care of her—scooping dry food into Coco's bowl, pouring new water into her dish, and changing her kitty litter. Last night he played with her a bit, which was unusual for him. He told Coco not to tell Mama but he never finished his fish classes in marine biology so he could start an internship and work with animals. Ted seemed more sad and quiet than happy lately. Coco loved Ted—even though he could be a real downer—but she was glad when he left and it was just Mama time.

Mama was coming home today. It was Friday, the beginning of

March, and still cold, but the sun streaming in through the window was warm. Coco rolled on her side, stretched her legs, and gazed outside, on the lookout for birds. A flash of red caught her eye. She sat up on her haunches, ears alert, whiskers trembling. In the adjacent wing across the way, on the balcony of a fourteenth-floor condo, Ted, wearing a red hoodie, paced back and forth, back and forth. *What's he doing home so early?* Coco tracked his moves, until finally, hypnotized by his pacing, she closed her eyes and promptly fell asleep.

After a while, partially awake, Coco opened her eyes, lifted her head, and spotted Ted still on his balcony, but this time, he was standing very still. When she woke the next time, she looked up to see if he was still there. He wasn't. She looked down and saw him sprawled on the pavement of the parking lot. Had he jumped and landed wrong? That happened to her sometimes. After a minute, she would stand up, shake herself, and walk away from the scene. He would probably get up in a minute.

A few minutes later, around four o'clock, Coco heard Mama's key in the lock. Mama came in, closed the door behind her, set down her luggage, and stood there, looking at Coco, who lifted her head, stood up, and stretched. Usually, when Mama came home, especially from a trip, she called out to Coco, her voice cheerful. But the last few times she returned home, she'd been unusually quiet, distracted. So this time, instead of waiting for Mama to come to her, Coco jumped down from the windowsill and padded over to greet Mama, winding around Mama's legs, rubbing her soft fur against Mama's rough wool pants. Coco loved these pants. They felt good against her skin, scratchy.

Mama picked Coco up and sat on the couch, kneading the top of Coco's head.

Coco meowed.

"What did you do all day, little one?"

Coco meowed, several times, recounting the details. *Sat in the sun. Drank some water. Lay down on the couch. Had a little snack…* Her meows rose an octave with each detail. "Wow," Mama said. "You were busy! Did you miss me?"

Coco thumped her head against Mama. "Meow, meow."

Mama sighed. She looked so sad. "Oh, Coco," she said. "I miss me too. I tell you to be happy with who you are, and I'm not taking my own advice. I'm amazed at how well you've accepted yourself, how fierce you are about being yourself and no one else, and here I am, so afraid. I can't stand it, and I don't know what to do."

She stood up, and set Coco down. "I'm going to take a nap." Mama kicked off her shoes, slid the afghan from the back of the couch, fluffed the pillows, and lay down. She curled on her side, facing Coco, and then tucked the afghan behind her legs.

Coco watched Mama for a minute, confused. *Hey! What's up with the naps? You know I'm all about a good nap, but this isn't normal for you. You're usually a ball of energy. You vacuum to relax. You text while you vacuum. You don't do naps.*

Mama pulled the afghan up under her chin.

Fine. I'll look out the window. Coco padded back to the windowsill, hopped up, and sat down. She could see lots of colored flashing lights below. *Hold up. What's going on?*

"Coco, come here!" Mama called from couch. "Lie down by me."

Coco's ears pricked up, but she couldn't move. *Not now,* Coco thought. *No way.* She could not take her eyes off the colored lights flashing in the parking lot below. *Something big is going on.* She stared, mesmerized by a big red fire truck, the ambulances, police cars, and all those pretty flashing lights, just like that laser toy that Mama chased her with. The sirens that usually accompanied the flashing lights were not on. No sound. She turned her head, angled it left, then right, following the pretty red flashers.

"Coco, what are you doing over there?" Mama stood up and walked over to the windowsill. She looked down and gasped. "Oh, my God!" she said. "I have to find out what's going on!"

Mama kissed the top of Coco's head and ran to the elevators. Things weren't looking good. *I hope it's not a fire. But what if it is? What if we have to leave?!* They'd had a false alarm before. She figured that was what Mama was so frightened of—a fire.

While Mama was gone, Coco paced around, looking for her favorite toy. If they had to leave the building, she and Mr. Mousie would be ready to go. She looked in her toy basket, under the couch. *Where is he? This is entirely too stressful. Mama!!*

A few minutes later, Mama walked in, tears streaming down her cheeks. She sat down on the couch, and patted her lap. That was Coco's cue for cuddle time. She jumped up and settled in. *What happened?* Coco tilted her head to the side.

"Oh, Coco, something terrible has happened."

Oh no. Am I going to lose another life?

"It's Ted."

Coco couldn't stand it anymore. *What? What?*

"Ted," Mama barely whispered, "That's Ted down there. He jumped."

I know. I saw him. But why are you crying?

"It's not like when *you* jump," Mama said. "Although even you couldn't survive a jump from that height. When people jump like that, they're very sad and troubled. It's rare for people to jump like that and not end their life. He didn't want to survive the jump and he didn't."

Wait. He's not getting up? He's not coming around anymore? He's not going to take his fish class?

Mama was really upset. "I had no idea he was even thinking about suicide. I've known him since I got you five years ago when he shared his dream of working with little animals. Remember that day? His vision? Starting an internship? I thought he was taking classes? If I'd known him longer, or better, maybe I would have realized..." She sat there, quiet, shocked, and held Coco for a while. Then she wiped her eyes.

He must have been sooo sad. I'm really gonna miss Ted.

"I don't think he could recognize that we all have the ability to change our lives. Remember we talked about how we can alter the outcome of our lives based on what we're thinking and feeling in our heads and hearts?"

Coco remembered. It had been a long time ago. Coco could tell Mama needed to talk, maybe for quite a while, so Coco jumped down to stretch and wake herself up—so she could be alert for Mama.

"Well, Ted, that poor troubled soul, did not understand," Mama said. "He lived with the belief that he could not change his life. All those negative things he believed about himself became his reality. I thought he was doing better. Apparently that reality was so difficult for him that the only option in his mind was to end his life."

Coco wanted to help Mama, but what could she do? Mama sat on the black leather couch, not moving, right next to the scratch on the armrest that Coco had left when she had long claws. Her arms hung at her sides as she stared toward her balcony. Coco circled around Mama's ankles, but Mama didn't seem to feel better. Coco stretched up with her paws on Mama's knees, then she sat back on her haunches, turned her head to the side, and studied Mama.

Mama looked the way Coco must have when she woke up after she had been spayed, when she couldn't understand why people wanted to fix what wasn't wrong. Kind of like Ted's boss and friends wanting him to be different from who he was. Mama had dark circles under her eyes, and she was chewing her lower lip. She did that sometimes.

I don't know how humans make it through each day, Coco thought. It was true that she was more complex and sophisticated than most animals, but she didn't think her life was as confusing as theirs seemed to be. *It must be really hard to be a human. For example, why would you jump off a high-rise balcony and not try to right yourself so that you would land on your feet?*

Coco meowed, and Mama kind of smiled to let her know she'd heard, but Mama usually reacted with more enthusiasm. Usually her eyes lit up, and she'd pick Coco up and say, "Come sit with me little one." Usually Coco could tell what Mama was thinking. But right now, when Coco looked in Mama's big brown eyes, she had no idea.

I'm a cat. Your cat. It's my job to take care of you and make you smile. She blinked at Mama. *But how? I don't know what to do.* So she leapt into Mama's lap, startling her. Mama jumped, attempting to come out of her reverie, but her hand fell limp on Coco's back, and she made no effort to scratch or pet her. It was a bit irritating.

Usually when Coco was irritated, she'd just leave, but this time, she knew Mama needed her, so she stayed where she was.

Coco didn't have to think about how to be a cat. But being a human seemed really hard. She curled up on Mama's lap and began to purr, going into a kind of trance, focusing hard on trying to make Mama feel better. After a while, Mama took a deep breath, and slowly began to rub the top of Coco's head between her ears, the way she loved. And they sat there, Mama and Coco, until Mama was ready to talk.

Mama took a deep breath, let it out, started to speak, then stopped, opened her mouth again, and said, "I never told you, Coco," Mama hesitated, "but I'm gay." Mama looked at Coco, head tilted, eyes questioning. "You probably have no idea what I'm talking about, do you?"

Coco bumped Mama with her head. *Go on.* Poor Mama. She felt so alone.

"I haven't told many people," Mama said, "because I've been afraid—almost like Ted. He had a dream to work with animals and never believed that he could. I've been afraid that if people really knew who I was, they wouldn't like me, or I'd lose my job. My biggest fear was that my family would disown me. It happens in a lot of families."

Not if you're a cat, Coco thought. *We're one hundred percent tolerant with some hissing as needed. Humans really have it rough. Their ability to reason isn't all it was cracked up to be. I need to help Mama.* She purred and purred, a steady hum, and finally, Mama let out a huge breath. Coco was getting through.

"I'm so glad I found you," Mama said, tears rolling down her cheeks. "I don't know what I'd do without you."

Coco buried her face in Mama's sweater. *I feel the same way.* She didn't remember her cat mama, but her human mama had always been her real mama. She was the absolute best mama Coco could imagine.

"Only very recently," Mama said, tears rolling down her cheeks, "did I learn to be honest with who I am, regardless of what others may think or feel about me. I'm beautiful and smart and compassionate, and I want to help others see themselves in all their worthiness. I want to help others live greater, more fulfilling, lives—just like I'm learning to do. I want to help people become more, to work and live with greater fulfillment."

Coco purred, content. She got it. She wanted to do her part too. Mama had always been the one helping Coco, but now the tables had turned. Mama had gone through a lot that day. Revealing more about herself to Coco and accepting herself had been a big deal for her, a real shift. Because Mama's life would be different, Coco's life would be different too. She was on Mama's team. And, as with any major, life-altering change, Coco lost another life. She had lived four lives by this point. Now she was down to five. She was a lot wiser, and it was time for her to do what she was here to do—help Mama by being there for her.

BECOME MORE:

- It's tough being human. Acceptance and being present for someone—just being there—can provide the space for acknowledgement and change.

- Coping with loss, defeat and failure is a part of life. The opposite of failure is resilience or the ability to get back up again. Allow your imagination to create Plan A, B, or C because there are always alternatives! Lean on people who believe in you and your vision as well. Positive support is contagious!

CHAPTER SIX
FOUR LIVES—FACING FEAR

COCO COULDN'T SEE a thing from her crate. Not one thing. She could hear though—the honking horns and rumbling engines of the cars speeding past on the highway, the music blaring from the odd car driving next to them, music that caused Mama to put her foot on the gas in an attempt to pull ahead, yelling, "Are you deaf?" The whole experience was unbearable. Coco was miserable, disoriented, and had no idea how long she'd be imprisoned in this plastic hellhole.

She meowed, really more a wail than a meow. *Enough!*

"It's going to be alright, Coco," Mama said. "We'll be at our new home soon."

They were moving to a new city for Mama's job, where they'd live in a temporary apartment until Mama found the perfect new home. At six years old, Coco hadn't had any say in the matter. She didn't want to move, and she certainly hadn't opted for this horrendous drive.

I'm not buying this "soon" business. She'd heard Mama talking to her mother on the phone a week or two before they'd left their beloved ninth-floor condo. Mama had said their new home was three hours away. Coco had an unclear idea about how far away three hours was, but it sounded like forever, and the drive was proving that it was, in fact, forever. At least it felt that way. She was hot, thirsty, and dizzy from anxiety and constant movement. Spots swam before her eyes. *You're in Mama's car,* she kept telling herself. *You're going to your new home. It's alright.* But it didn't feel alright. She needed water. "Meoooowww."

"Just a minute, little one." Mama signaled and eased the car to the side of the highway, gravel crunching underneath the tires as they stopped. She turned off the engine, and opened her door. Ding ding ding ding.

Is Mama leaving me? The hair in Coco's ears stood on end as she listened, straining to hear what Mama was doing. She heard feet on crushed rocks. Then, *phew,* Mama opened the back door and unlatched the wire gate on her crate. Too sick to make a break for it, Coco sat still while Mama opened a bottle of water, poured some onto her fingers, and wet Coco's nose.

"I don't want you to become dehydrated," Mama said.

Whatever that means. Mama wet Coco's nose a few more times, and then picked up Coco's cage, set it on the passenger seat, slid behind the wheel, buckled up, and pulled back onto the highway. For the rest of the drive, Mama stopped every fifteen minutes to wet Coco's nose. Even with Mama stopping to cool her off, Coco's head pounded, she couldn't think straight, and the rest of the trip passed in a blur of confusion and misery.

Next thing Coco knew, she was in Mama's arms, covered with

her blankie, Mama rubbing between her ears. After a while, Coco could breathe. *There we go. That's better.* She peeked out from the blanket. She and Mama were sitting on the floor next to her crate, and her water dish was filled with cool, clean, delicious water. Her toy box was in the corner; the black leather couch backed against the far wall. Coco felt better. *Some of the things are the same, but the house is different.* She burrowed into her blankie and closed her eyes. She'd made it.

❧ ❧

When Mama went to work that Monday, Coco felt a little nervous being in her new home by herself. The new apartment was on the ground floor, so Coco could look up at the birds instead of down, the way she had from their condo on the Gold Coast. She looked outside through a huge opening in the wall that Mama said was a sliding glass door, whatever that meant. What she saw was a gigantic new perspective to the world outside, a large, drooping willow, and a wooden bridge spanning the shores of a small pond with a fountain.

Sitting before the glass, scoping out the birds, Coco zeroed in on one with a red head and a gray body, hopping on a tree branch. Coco sat taller, whiskers forward, eyes focused, at one with the bird. At just the right moment, she'd pounce. Even without her long claws, she could take the bird. She knew it, because she dreamt this outcome. She was totally confident.

But then… wait, what's that? Can birds swim? Huge honking things floating on the water! At first she was confused as to why anybody would voluntarily be in the water, but quickly, another scarier thought dawned on her. *These birds are enormous. Brown and white with green heads. And mean! I can tell by their beady eyes.* She tried to arch her back and hiss. She wanted to let loose one of her super loud meows, but she couldn't. She sat, frozen. She couldn't stop shaking. *These birds are not friendly. These birds will attack me. Those large beaks will go for my eyes.*

She had to get out of there—*one, two, three, can't move, four… still frozen. Try again, one, two, three*—and with closed eyes, Coco took off! Into the bedroom, straight into the closet. Heart pounding, she peered out the door. *No sign of the monster birds. I've outwitted them. Of course. But I'm not going back out there.* She began pacing, past Mama's work slacks, her fancy shirts, her fuzzy bathrobe hanging on the back of the door. The closet smelled like Mama, comforting, calm, safe. Finally, when no birds came, Coco curled up behind the luggage and slept. Hours later, when she heard Mama's key in the door, she tore out of the closet to see her. Mama never knew Coco had been in the closet, and Coco certainly wasn't going to tell her. She had her dignity after all.

🐾 🐾

Three months later, Coco was still running to the closet every day after Mama left, still hiding all day, keeping her fear hidden from Mama. Every day, as she sat in the closet, she dreamed about how she would soon face her enemy. *What if I sprung out of this closet, roared at those birds, and scared them silly?* Coco thought. *What if I ran out to the living room, pulled the cord on the curtains with my teeth so the opening in the wall would be covered, preventing those birds from seeing me?*

Coco tried to act out the "what ifs" so she could take her life back, but pretty soon she'd be down the wrong "what if" path. *What if those big birds aren't scared of my roar? What if they can peck their way through the curtains?*

One Friday, as she sat shivering in Mama's closet as usual, huddled on top of a moving box, surrounded by her blankie, she heard someone in the house. Had the geese, as Mama called them, come into the house? It couldn't be. She had to calm down. *Maybe the woman who feeds me when Mama travels?* No, it was too late for her, she came in the mornings. *Could it be Mama? Oh, please, let it be Mama.* But it couldn't be Mama. She didn't get home from work until evening. Plus, Mama always called from the front door unless she was in the middle of a phone call or a text. Or maybe it was one of those days Mama worked at home, going out only to run an errand? Yes, maybe it could be Mama.

Ears perked up, whiskers vibrating, Coco pictured the geese waddling through the house, those horrifying serrated orange beaks leading the way, clawed feet paddling down the hall, into the bedroom, approaching the closet door. Coco sat back farther, scrunched down even more, eyes unblinking, intent on the sunbeam shining through the eight-inch gap of the open door.

Waiting, waiting. Hold up. Geese don't smell like Armani. Mama opened the door, phone in her right hand. She peered in the closet. "There you are, weasel."

Mama! Coco tried to jump down to greet her, but she was still so paralyzed with fear, she couldn't move.

"C'mon Coco," Mama said. "Let's play."

Nope. Still can't move. Maybe it's better if I just stay where I am.

"What's wrong?" Mama asked. "Wait, stay right there, I'll be right back."

No, Coco thought, shaking head to foot. *Don't go.* She pointed her short tail, the way she did when she was frightened or angry. And then Mama came back and kneeled down, waving Coco's purple ribbon.

Totally unfair, Coco thought, relaxing a little. If anything could lure her out of her hiding place it was that ribbon. Or dinner. But then she heard it. *A honk! Had Mama let the geese in with her? Didn't Mama understand the danger?*

Quick Mama, Coco meowed. *Come in here with me and hold me, because I do not like those geese. All I can see are flapping wings. Those beaks. My funeral!* Shivering, she imagined a procession of neighbors, walking through the street, carrying a small box, standing around her grave. "Coco was a good cat," they'd say. *I was a lot more than that,* Coco thought. *I AM a lot more.* But she was too scared to come up with anything better. *And wait, I'm not dead yet.* Although surely the fear of these geese had cost her another life.

Mama's voice pulled her out of her terror. "What is it, weasel?" Mama peered through the hanging pant legs at Coco, and suddenly, her eyes lit up. "The geese!" Mama said. "That's what's going on. Why didn't you tell me?" Mama reached for Coco, picked her up, held her close to her heart. Coco burrowed her head into Mama's fuzzy sweater. "Ssshh," Mama said. "Ssshh." Coco loved it when Mama held her, calming her down.

"Come with me," Mama said.

Well, really, Coco thought. *Where else would I go? (A) I'm caught in Mama's death grip, and (B) I'm too scared to move.*

Mama tiptoed down the hall and into the living room. "It's okay," she kept saying.

When Mama reached the big opening in the wall, she rapped her knuckles against it. "It's glass," Mama said. "An invisible door." She rapped again. "It's okay. They can't get to you."

Slowly, cautiously, Coco raised her head just a smidge to peek over Mama's forearm. *Fierce geese on the grass! Plucking up grass with their feet, itching for a fight.* Coco buried her face in Mama's sweater, her eyes squeezed shut so the geese wouldn't see her. *This was how you show me your love, Mama? Is this another lesson in personal growth? Not the time or place.*

"Nothing's going to happen, Coco," Mama said. "They can't even hear you. All those months, you were hiding for nothing." Mama nuzzled Coco's neck with her nose.

Coco loved that. She took a breath. "They can't get to you," Mama said. "Look." Coco turned her head, opened her eyes, looked out at the trees and the grass and the geese going about their business. And then she got it. They really couldn't get through.

From that day on, for the rest of their time in the apartment, she staked her claim by the door, taking in the grass and the trees, stretching out to sleep in a sunbeam, knowing she was totally safe. She'd lost yet another life over those geese, but she had four lives left. And she was getting wiser.

BECOME MORE:

- Fears create new barriers that cripple our self-esteem and prevent us from moving toward our goals.

- Overcome the temptation to hide and play small. Your fear is only based on potentially excelling in uncharted territory, which could be your success! Yet most people are fearful because they assume that uncharted territory will result in failure. Remember, "Says who?" And throw away your defective crystal ball!

CHAPTER SEVEN
THREE LIVES—DENIAL AND STAGNATION

MAMA DIDN'T WAIT very long after the geese incident before finding their new permanent home—a gorgeous condo with gray carpeting and black-and-white details, the color of Coco's fur, which Coco saw as a sign that the new condo was their perfect home. Coco was seven years old. They had a new home. She learned so much with every life lost. Now it's time to make what's left really count.

This time when Mama moved them, Coco knew ahead of time. She was no fool. That moving vibe was in the air. Then a team of humans in sweaty clothes infiltrated the space, packing boxes and hauling furniture to a big truck parked in front of the apartment. They were taking all Mama's stuff—the leather couch where Coco snuggled with Mama, the TV—but so far had left all of Coco's personal belongings. Coco perched on top of her cat tower in the living room, watching the movers, keeping her eye out for that plastic hellhole of a crate Mama put her in last time.

"Kitty, kitty," one nice lady said, as she walked past Coco to pick up her bed. *Her bed!!!* Coco hissed at her, but Mama scolded, "Coco! Be nice! Stop hissing!"

Please, Coco thought. *You really don't have to take that tone with me in front of strangers.* Coco stopped hissing and flattened the mover with her cool stare. She had her dignity.

"Wait," Mama said to the mover. "Could you please leave that bed?"

There you go, Mama.

"I'll take it in my car," Mama said to the mover, "along with the rest of Coco's things—her toys, her bowl."

Okay, so Mama's trying to be nice. Whatever. Coco was seriously miffed. Mama had been just a bit too worked up about the move, a bit too snippy lately. *I'm the one who should be snippy. Am I ever going to have a say in these moves? Or get to decide how I spend my nine lives?* Seriously. Every move, every big scary change, began a new life, and cost her an old one. *Enough with the self-pity,* Coco told herself. She bent her head and licked her shoulder, cleaning the moving dust from her fur.

Hey that's MY bowl! Coco hissed as one of the movers grabbed her food dish. Mama stepped in again, took the dish, thanked him, and put the dish in her pile by the door. Mama had just washed the bowl with some new stinky soap, so the car wouldn't smell like food. But now when Mama fed her—God knew when, because who knew where they were going and when they'd get there—that bowl was going to smell too clean. *Soap for dinner? Ugh.*

Coco jumped off the couch and padded into the bedroom, springing lightly on her paws to seek refuge under the bed. Maybe catch a nap before the movers stormed the room to dismantle her sleeping quarters. Coco crawled under the frame, lay on her side, and stretched out. *Ahhh. So much better.*

"Coco," Mama called. "Coco, come play with me."

Oh no, Coco thought. *I know what you're trying to do, Mama. Lure me into the crate. I'm staying right where I am.*

"Come play with me," Mama called again.

Seriously? What kind of fool do you take me for?

"Coco," Mama sang, just as Coco spied a big fat work boot next to the bed, ruling out naptime. Where should she go next? She had to move fast, because now three pairs of boots surrounded her. Coco rolled over, sprang from under the bed, and tore into the living room, where Mama stood, wadding a piece of paper in her hand. "Look, Coco." She nodded to a long, flat box, maybe for their printer?

I could crawl in and sleep there, and—

Heads up! A paper ball flew past as Mama tossed it in the box. Mama was taking a break to play with her. *That's more like it.* Coco twitched her nose, sniffed the box, set one paw down carefully, then the other. The cardboard was slippery, but after one step, two, she got the hang of it. She could see the white paper ball at the back of the box, just a few more inches, and... Mama closed the flaps. It was dark. Really dark.

"It's not for long," Mama said. "Only thirty minutes. I'm sorry to lock you in this box. Just hang tight."

What's up with that? Making me think you're going to haul me around in the crate and then pulling a switcheroo? You tricked me, and I really don't appreciate it. I'm never moving again.

❖ ❖

But apparently she was. Only a few years after they settled into the new condo, Mama started dating, and, almost right away, the two of them decided to build a gigantic house together. What was with Mama? Nobody asked Coco if she was okay with moving so soon, with being part of a new family. It was just like her operations all over again. Big change, new life. She felt as though she didn't exist. The way things were going, she soon wouldn't.

Mama and her new partner were so excited about building their new home. The whole enterprise was pretty hard to deal with—crazy, frenetic energy. In fact, Mama and her new special person seemed a little *too* excited, too enthusiastic—especially Mama, first burying herself in designing the house, then in building the house, and now finishing the house. Chewing her lip, speeding out to the home improvement store, squinting her eyes at the computer, leaning into the screen, scrolling through page after page of designs for faucets, sinks, drawer pulls, molding, and appliances. Coco didn't think Mama's relationship with her partner was deep and true, like hers and Mamas. She was so busy that she overlooked the little fights, the differences, the growing distance between her and her partner. Clearly, Coco observed, Mama thought the house would solve all their problems.

Coco heard Mama telling one of her friends on the phone that she thought something was not right with the relationship, that they were two very different people, in fact, but that she was in too deep with the house, they were too far along. Plus, she'd sunk a lot of money into the place. Coco heard other friends urging Mama to get out, to cut her losses and bail, but Mama wouldn't listen. When she hung up the phone after talking with one of her friends, she would sit still for a few minutes, staring at the phone, deep in thought. Mama had always been brave, so Coco didn't know why she didn't have the guts to just put on the brakes. Coco didn't think it was just about money, something else was going on.

Unlike Mama, Coco didn't believe that when they moved into their beautiful new home in the upscale but rural suburbs everything would be fine. But what could Coco do?

🐾 🐾

One night before they moved, Mama came home from her partner's house, unlocked the front door, stepped inside, and immediately pulled off her shoes, then, quickly, wobbling on one leg, one sock, then switched legs to remove the other. She dropped both socks by the door and headed, bare feet on deep carpet, to the kitchen. Returning with a white laundry bag, Mama stooped down next to her socks, and pinched them between her thumb and index finger.

Eyes wide, she whispered, "Coco, look at all this dog hair. My socks—completely covered." Mama's partner spent most of her time at Coco and Mama's house, leaving her dog with a friend. On the few occasions Mama had gone over there, she hadn't been wearing socks, had just slipped off her shoes and gone barefoot, so she hadn't noticed the hair. Now she was clearly upset. Coco couldn't blame her—dog hair was revolting.

Mama dropped the socks in the bag. Coco pranced over to get a closer look at the socks. She peered in the bag, arched her back, and hissed. *Dog fur! Disgusting!*

"It's her dog," Mama whispered, as though her partner could hear her. "It's like I dust-mopped the floor with my socks." She pulled on the drawstring bag to shut the bag. "I can't do it, Coco. I can't live with all that hair and the barking and the jumping! I'm a nervous wreck!"

I'm with you there, Coco thought. Maybe Mama would back out?

Mama picked up the bag and strode to the bedroom stabbing the air with her free hand as she spoke, Coco following, concerned. "I'm totally freaked out," Mama said. "I can't even breathe. I have dog hair in my nose, on my pants. Everywhere." Coco trailed Mama into the bathroom, belly flopped on the cool tile, and lay there, front and back legs splayed, while Mama dropped her pants into the laundry bag, pushed the bag away from Coco, and stepped into the shower. "I'll have to take those pants to the dry cleaners," Mama said. "They'll probably fire me as a customer."

Mama, Coco thought, *let's get down to what's really bothering you. It's not your partner's dog you're worried about, or the dog hair. It's your partner you have doubts about moving in with.* Coco blasted her thoughts at Mama so she'd understand the real problem.

"Anyway," Mama said, calling to Coco through the steam. "Your new stepmom was apologizing all over the place."

Stepmom? I don't think so. Coco thought harder.

"She felt terrible," Mama said, "but she said there's absolutely no way she can pick up hair every five minutes, which is what it would take to keep her house hair-free. I don't want her to feel she has to vacuum all the time. I don't want to either. But how can I live like that? We're too different, this isn't going to work."

Now you're getting it.

"I mean, seriously," Mama said, "How am I supposed to live with dog hair?"

Or maybe not. Coco would have to try again later. How could she concentrate with all this talk about dog hair?

"It will get in my food," Mama went on, "on my suits. I can't go into a meeting or stand up front in a conference room looking like a damn hairball."

Calm down, Mama. Calm down. But then Coco realized *she* was breathing rapidly and was in no position to calm Mama down. *Dog hair?! No way am I moving into the new house.*

❧ ❧

On moving day, Mama and Coco got to the new house first. *Wow!* It really was a palace, even grander than the Gold Coast palace, or the condo they'd just left behind. There were so many windows to look out of and sunbeams to lie in—not that she'd get any peace when Mama's partner came with the D.O.G. And the yard was huge! Coco perched on the arm of her beloved leather couch in the great room, watching the world outside. She sat up straight on her hind legs, batting her paws, as though she could actually make contact with the birds hopping on the grass. But of course she couldn't. They were on the other side of the glass. This was too much. Coco sprang from her seat and ran to the back door, where she meowed for Mama to let her out. Mama didn't come. She meowed again. *Let me out, Mama.* But no Mama. What was the point? Mama wouldn't let her out anyway. Coco was an inside cat.

Coco yawned, then took off to explore the other bedrooms and office and the loft far above the great room. Halfway into the master bedroom, she stopped. There was a huge bed! *Where am I supposed to sleep?* She wanted to sleep with Mama, curled up behind her knees, but things were different now, and Coco had to share Mama. But Coco didn't want to share Mama with anyone.

Plus the bedroom had a faint smell of another animal. It most definitely was not another cat! She could handle that. *This will never work.* Coco hopped up to the sill to sulk. She wanted nothing to do with these beings. Nothing to do with this house. How was she supposed to make the most of her lives if she spent every spare minute getting used to different circumstances? And once again, had she been consulted? Mama and her partner seemed to make all the decisions. If that's how it was going to be, why should Coco bother to chime in?

When she finished sulking, Coco trotted to check out the kitchen, which had shiny tile floors with a door onto a deck. *Darn!* Those white cabinets were high for her to get on the top of before being discovered by the dog.

About an hour later, Coco sat minding her business, perched on the bar stool by the kitchen counter, when Mama's partner finally arrived at this new "home," opened the front door, and called out. Coco let out her breath. She had known this moment had to come, she had known it ever since Mama had come home that day with dog hair-covered socks. She knew that even though Mama was freaked out about the dog hair, the dog would be part of their life, invading it, along with his mama. And here he was. The scent hit Coco right away. Sweat and oily dog skin, every smell in the yard and worse clinging to his fur. The dog barked. Coco stayed on her perch. *Nice and high. Out of his reach. Safe.* She had never seen a dog up close before, except at the shelter, when she had been stuck in her crate, and she had only seen those dogs out of the corner of her eye. She wasn't anxious to meet this one face to face.

The dog was nearer. What was that noise? He was sniffing like Mama did when she had a cold, only one hundred times louder and faster, and then he stopped sniffing and started running, skidding around the corner, nails clicking on the tile kitchen floor, tail wagging wildly, whining with joy. Barking with glee to meet his new fuzzy stepsister.

Mama promised her a proper introduction, to allow Coco and the dog time to get used to each other and ease into their relationship. But this, Coco decided, was anything but proper. There he was, Beast. Mama and her partner the Dog Lady stood at the kitchen door, out of breath from following the dog. Coco regarded Mama coolly, then turned back to the crisis at hand—Beast was barking at her bar stool! She wasn't safe. He could jump right up and grab her between his huge, sharp teeth. Coco arched her back, ears at attention, and hissed, her mouth open, teeth flashing, channeling the wrath of her ancestors, her sisters in the wild, runts of the litter around the globe.

The dog jumped up, his paws resting on the seat edge of the stool. Coco batted his snout with one paw, then whacked the side of his face with the other. He sat perfectly still, raised his eyebrows as though confused, and turned his head toward Mama and Dog Lady, who were watching and laughing from the sidelines. "They seem to be just playing," Mama's partner said.

Not getting any help from Dog Lady, Beast turned back to Coco, who sat on her hind legs and batted him with one paw then the next, one, two, the dog swinging his head from side to side until he was fed up and snapped his head back and went for her throat. True, it was a soft approach, more playful than fierce, but Coco was furious. She opened her mouth and meowed, launched herself at his face, clung to it as he howled and fell back, rolling on the floor.

Mama's partner rushed to the sink, pulled out the kitchen faucet sprayer and nailed the tangled two of them.

Hey! HE started it!

A few minutes later, after the dog had been temporarily banished from the kitchen, Mama sat on the floor, back against the cabinets, and rubbed Coco down with a thick, fuzzy bath towel. "I never dreamed it would be this bad," she said. "A period of transition, perhaps? *Transition? I'm terrified Mama!* Coco, her world forever changed, is left with three lives remaining.

🐾 🐾

There were three ducks next door. Coco spied on them when she sunned herself on the sill of the living room window. Three ducks— large, medium, and small—that never moved. Ever. They wore clothes like Mama wore, only not as stylish. They hid their webbed feet in yellow rain boots. Matching yellow capes covered their wings. Their bills peeked out from bright yellow bonnets. Mama said they were ceramic. Coco didn't know what that meant, but she knew it wasn't good. "Damn ceramic ducks… why do people dress them up?" Mama would say, when she'd pick Coco up from the sill. "Don't waste your time, Coco."

Mama's partner told her she wanted to buy some ceramic ducks to place in their front yard and for a minute Mama believed her. Then she started laughing. Coco knew Mama's partner was teasing her, but Coco didn't get the joke. Still, when Mama and her partner laughed, it made her feel safe, especially because it happened less and less. They lived in a beautiful subdivision, but it was in the country. Out in the middle of nowhere, Mama said. "I had no idea it would be so isolated here," she told Coco, burying her nose in Coco's fluffy neck. "But it's too late now." She sounded sad. Mama's friends teased her about moving to the country. They said she was taking a step backward, but Coco thought Mama was staying in the same place. Stuck.

🐾 🐾

Five years had gone by since they'd moved to their house, and Coco, now nearly twelve years old, still loved watching the birds and pretending she was outside. At least the birds looked happy, unlike Coco. Sad and feeling left out of Mama's big decisions, Coco lost yet another life, leaving her with only two lives left. She'd felt trapped in the house from the beginning, trapped in the house with the smelly D.O.G. And finally, after five years, Mama felt trapped too. Mama's friends kept asking her why she stayed if she was so unhappy, and Mama would answer with a blank stare, because she didn't know why. And she didn't know how to get out, which Coco didn't understand. Mama had used her free will when she moved in with her partner. Why couldn't she take advantage of her free will and move out?

That night, when Mama came home from work, she set down her briefcase, hung up her coat, and sat down by Coco. She didn't say anything, just scratched Coco behind her ears. They both sat there, together, staring at the birds. Coco had never liked change. She hadn't liked her operations. She'd hated living in this house. But Mama had taught her that change is constant. And when Coco thought about it, some changes in her life had been good—moving in with Mama, moving to the temporary apartment, then moving into their beautiful condo. Maybe it was a good thing that Mama hadn't been able to sell the condo and had started renting it to a nice family. Coco dreamed of moving back to their beautiful condo. She could take action in her mind, visualize living there once again. *Life with just me and Mama there was wonderful.*

Sadly, Mama had settled. She thought the relationship was as good as it gets, and getting out didn't seem to be an option in the foreseeable future. *Not an option? That was odd—since when did the Universe limit humans on choice? Since when did Mama?* Even in

Coco's little world, she found ways to have fun, found total joy with a rubber band, a Q-tip! Spiders! Sunbeams!

Coco nudged Mama's leg with her head, and crawled on to her lap. As she had countless times before, she thought hard, picturing the movers putting the leather couch in the truck, felt how it used to feel, she and Mama living together in their condo, pictured Mama and her partner listing the house, sad but relieved that they'd finally started communicating, talking about something that mattered, finally exploring their options.

Coco knew if Mama secretly wanted change but couldn't see how to make it happen, the Universe might very well smack her upside the head and make her change. Mama sighed. She'd been getting sick lately, run down from stress. Her work had slowed down, fueled both from her depression and the economic climate, which made it even more frightening for her to consider making a change. And most of all, Coco knew, Mama couldn't bear to tell her family and friends that her life and her relationship—the one she'd had such high hopes for—had deteriorated so badly. Coco snuggled into Mama's lap and purred. She pictured Mama happy—in a new home with plenty of work, feeling fit and healthy. And for a minute, the briefest minute, she thought she saw Mama's lips curve up just a little bit. But just as quickly, the smile was gone, and Coco was no longer able to get through to her. She was just too sad.

Then one day, just as in Coco's dream, the movers came, and Coco hid in the corner behind the couch, where she often took refuge from the dog. Were they leaving? Was Mama finally taking action? She kept an eye out for her crate. Or a box. But Mama wasn't the one who was moving. It was her partner. That night, after Coco finished her dinner, she padded into the living room to find

Mama gazing out the window at the empty driveway, her partner's car gone forever.

BECOME MORE:

- Feeling left out of the big picture leads to apathy, disengagement, and fear of making a necessary change. Communication is crucial, with everyone involved.

- When we deny ourselves what we truly want, we are settling. Take inventory by asking yourself these questions:

  * In what aspect(s) of your life are you settling? (Career, relationships, lifestyle, finances, etc.)

  * Why are you afraid to walk away from these situations?

  * What could happen if you stopped settling?

  * What new beliefs will help you manifest the ideal situation?

  * What tiny steps can you take to move toward this new goal?

CHAPTER EIGHT
TWO LIVES—TAKING ACTION

WHEN MAMA REALIZED the love of her life had found someone new, she went through a deep depression. "I feel like such a failure," she told Coco. Trying to cheer her up, Coco cuddled with Mama, meowed in conversational tones, and raced around the room, which had always made Mama laugh. Not anymore, though. Coco couldn't get Mama to crack a smile.

After a while, Coco just stayed by Mama's side as she rode waves of emotions, from denial to anger to sadness, until finally, after many, many months, Mama realized that the change had been inevitable. She and her partner had both been unhappy, and finally, her partner had taken the first step. In hindsight, it was the greatest gift her partner had ever given Mama—freedom.

Feeling a bit better, Mama realized that putting the house up for sale would become the start of a new beginning. Her renters had moved out of the condo as well. So she listed her condo for sale or lease. Mama wanted to sell both places, pack up, grab Coco, and move out of state. She wanted to run away. At the time, she had no idea how difficult the housing market had become.

But three and a half years after Mama's partner left, the condo remained vacant, and the house was still on the market—both dwellings incurring price drop after price drop—during the most financially devastating period for real estate in recent history. In those three and a half years, Mama and Coco lived in the big house—alone.

☙ ☙

Coco was pretty fed up. True, they had the house to themselves, but Mama didn't know how she could pay the bills, keep up with the yard work, make the house neat and pretty for possible buyers, and still find time to play with Coco. Mama could never make it as a realtor. Coco had been watching her get the house ready to show for three years, every time her realtor called. And no sale. For three years, Mama had been lighting her vanilla candles. *What was it with humans and waxy fire things?* And baking her cookies. *How can the smell of cookies SELL a house? Are humans that simple?* Three years of making sure the toys were put away, of Coco spending evenings and weekends in her second home—the closet.

The house wasn't cheap. No one had offered a bid high enough for Mama, who kept saying, "I'm not going to lose money on this house." They hadn't lost a dime yet. But they hadn't made one either. And Mama was getting seriously frightened that she'd never sell.

Coco was at her wit's end. Mama was edgy and miserable. Sometimes when Coco meowed, Mama snapped, "Coco ssshh, damn it!! I can't hear myself think." Mama never used to speak to her like that.

If Coco were in charge of showing the house, she'd take an entirely different approach, a formal one. Of course, she was born formal—her tuxedo coat, her paws like white gloves—she knew how to treat people with class. Usually, when the realtor rang the doorbell Mama answered it and let everyone in. But in Coco's fantasy, Mama would be out. Somewhere. *I would make sure she was not home so I could lead the house tour!*

How differently I would conduct the process if she only LET me! The realtor would ring the bell and wait to let herself and the prospective buyers into the house. "Coco," she'd call. "May we come in?" Coco would wait a minute or two, setting her own pace, sauntering into the foyer, her little tail standing straight up. The realtor would introduce everyone to Coco, but Coco would keep her distance, meowing for them to follow. She wouldn't rub against their legs. She wouldn't hiss. She had a mission, to sell the house. After introductions, the realtor would sweep her hand (ungloved), and say, "Coco, lead the way."

Coco would set off for the kitchen—at a brisk yet elegant pace—where she'd hop to the counter and nudge first the coffee cups next to the freshly brewed pot, then the spoons, creamer, and sugar (*with silver tongs*). People seemed to calm down when drinking coffee, which Coco couldn't understand, because a few minutes after they'd had a cup, she noticed that they became quite twitchy. Still, Coco wanted her prospective buyers happy. She wanted them to picture waking up in the morning in her house, pouring coffee into their pretty mugs, relaxing in this bright, cheery kitchen.

In Coco's fantasy, people viewing the house wouldn't flinch when she jumped on the counter. They wouldn't gasp at a cat leading the way. And when she'd pat the cookie plate, urging them to take a snack, they wouldn't panic because her tuxedo fur rarely shed and the snacks were displayed invitingly. In her scenario, she would nod to the candle on the kitchen table. She included the candle as a concession to Mama, who swore it worked wonders. *Though, by that logic, the house would have been sold if it worked, right? Wrong!*

Still, Mama had built the house, so in Coco's fantasy, she let Mama keep the candle burning.

Then, with cups in hand, a cookie on a plate, the guests would follow Coco as she sauntered with authority and style into the great room and leapt onto the couch, landing perfectly and inviting her guests to sit down on the puffy cushions. In her fantasy, they understood. They sat. Now and then, someone either wouldn't understand her invitation to sit or they would refuse to sit, and Coco would veto the sale, meowing to the realtor, who would hurry the people along and out the door. In Coco's fantasy, it was usually winter, so she'd jump off the couch, hop over to the fireplace, and stretch out, rolling on her back, squirming on the floor—*heaven*—to let the people know how comfy the room could be.

Then she'd curl up and pretend to sleep, letting the guests sit, relax, sip their coffee, nibble their cookies. She wanted them to talk about the house. Since most humans didn't think she understood them, Coco would gather intel with her eyes closed, gaining insight into how to close the deal.

After about ten minutes, Coco would stretch, stand up, and lead the guests to the bedroom. They always loved that room. "Oohh, ahhh," they'd say, and they'd make a huge offer the same day. One thing Coco would avoid at all costs—putting Mama in the closet with a sign and picture on the door reading "Keep Out." True, Mama meant no harm when she hid Coco in that prison. She was just trying to sell the house and to provide some privacy for Coco, but Coco was absolutely clear—in her fantasy, Mama could go shopping, she could work in the yard or take off on a sales trip, but no one—no one—would live in the bedroom closet.

🐾 🐾

When Mama gave motivational seminars to sales people, she walked them through an exercise called Clarity through Contrast. She used a "T" chart to illustrate how to manifest what you want in your life, or, as Mama had explained to Coco, how thoughts become things. Mama learned about the tool when she earned her certification in Michael Losier's Law of Attraction course. The bottom line—if you're not getting the outcomes you want, you have to change your thinking. Change your thinking, change your outcomes.

In Coco's opinion, Mama needed to practice the exercise herself. Somehow, Mama was picturing an outcome that created another negative—she'd never lose money on the house—and she was sending that outcome into the Universe, which was obliging by not selling the house!

How could Coco get through to Mama? She tried blasting her with thoughts, the way she sometimes did, but Mama had a mental wall up, it seemed. If Mama were a cat, she would know what Coco was thinking, let alone saying. Coco closed her eyes and thought hard about what to do. When Coco was hungry, she pictured Mama opening the orange IAMS bag, her own ears pricking up, running into the kitchen. And almost every time, Mama would call her for breakfast or dinner or a snack. So, Coco thought, if she imagined pictures of what she was trying to say to Mama, maybe Mama might see them and understand.

So for three days, Coco followed Mama around picturing the "T" chart with all her might, hoping Mama would see it in her own mind. Three days. But Mama was so consumed with fear, worry, and negative outcomes that Coco couldn't get through. Her head ached from trying. *Please, Mama, pay attention!* Finally, one evening, while Coco and Mama were watching *Animal Planet*—Coco stretched out on her stomach, Mama curled up under an afghan—Mama sat up, pointed the remote at the TV, and clicked mute. "The 'T' chart," she said. "I need to make a 'T' chart."

Hallelujah! Coco raised her head and peered at Mama, then dropped her head down between her paws with relief.

Mama rushed into her office, returning at full speed with a legal pad and two sharp pencils. She plopped down on the couch, planted her feet on the glass coffee table, and drew a large "T" on the pad. Coco scooted over to Mama. Draping her paws across Mama's leg, she watched Mama write.

Across the top of the paper, Mama wrote, "I am in the process of attracting the ideal home buyer." On the left side of the "T," Mama started listing all the wrong types of buyers who had been walking through the door.

"Buyers not ready to purchase," she said as she wrote. "Buyers who can't qualify for a loan."

The more Mama wrote, the angrier she got—swearing and pressing so hard on her pencil it almost snapped in two. At one point, she slapped the pad on the table, and said, "What's the damn point?" Coco couldn't let Mama give up. She crawled onto her lap to provide support.

After a minute, Mama picked up the pad and started writing again. "The fun part's coming up," Mama said with determination.

Coco purred and purred.

Finally Mama sighed, and rolled her shoulders back. "Halfway there," she said.

Her list of buyers she didn't want looked like this:

I am in the process of attracting the ideal home buyer.	
Buyers not ready to purchase	
Buyers who can't qualify for a loan	
Buyers with an objection to privacy	
Buyers with kids too young to appreciate house layout and yard limitations	
Buyers who are just looking	
Buyers with contingencies or property to sell	
Buyers with unrealistic opening offer	
Buyers who want/need 4 bedrooms	
Buyers who expect a finished basement	
Buyers who don't like contemporary homes	
Buyers who don't want a corner lot	
Buyers who want/need a 3-car garage	

After a minute, Mama pressed pencil to paper, and resumed writing. Coco knew the drill. For every statement on the left side of the paper, Mama had to rewrite the statement on the right side, rephrasing it, giving it a positive spin. If she left the statement as a negative—"buyers not ready" and "buyers who can't qualify"—the Universe would hear "not ready" and "can't qualify," and that's the type of buyers

Mama would attract. One by one, Mama rewrote every statement, getting more and more excited. Eventually, her chart looked like this:

I am in the process of attracting the ideal home buyer.	
Buyers not ready to purchase	Buyers who are ready to purchase
Buyers who can't qualify for a loan	Buyers prequalified for $300k
Buyers with an objection to privacy	Buyers who like the corner lot and one adjacent neighbor
Buyers with kids too young to appreciate house layout and yard limitations	Buyers who love a first-floor master bedroom and entertaining layout
Buyers who are just looking	Buyers who are done looking
Buyers with contingencies or property to sell	Buyers with nothing to sell or need to relocate
Buyers with unrealistic opening offer	Buyers with realistic, value-based offer
Buyers who want/need 4 bedrooms	Buyers who see 3 bedrooms as a good fit
Buyers who expect a finished basement	Buyers who want a basement for storage
Buyers who don't like contemporary homes	Buyers who love a contemporary/classy home
Buyers who don't want a corner lot	Buyers who see the corner lot as an advantage
Buyers who want/need a 3-car garage	Buyers with 2 cars who find the garage just fine

When she finished rewriting the statements, Mama crossed out the negative statements on the left. Then she held up her chart. "Ta da!" She scooped Coco up and hugged her. "We did it!"

Coco plopped her head down and held the back of it with one of her paws. *Yeah, and my head is killing me. I need a drink.* Jumping off Mama's lap, she trotted into the kitchen, and lapped at her fresh, cool water. *Ahhh. Much better.* The throbbing eased a bit, and Coco padded back to the living room, hopped onto the couch, and curled up in Mama's lap.

"I need to write a paragraph about the ideal buyer," Mama said. "Someone who would really love this home and is easy to work with." She scribbled away and finally read her statement to Coco.

"I'm in the process of attracting the ideal buyer for my home at 555 Crestview Lane who is ready to purchase, prequalified for a loan, loves the corner lot with only one neighbor, and has been looking for a first-floor master bedroom. A buyer or family who needs the extra room for their older kids, visiting grandkids, or guests, so three bedrooms plus the loft is plenty, who wants a contemporary and classy home with a beautiful layout to entertain, a two-car garage, and a basement for storage. I'm in the process of attracting an ideal buyer who submits a realistic, value-based offer."

When she finished reading, Mama seemed happier, lighter. "Coco," she said. "Listen to me. I'm going to make a very bold prediction. If I have to lose money on this house, then that amount times one hundred will be my net worth some day."

Oh, boy! Mama, you're realigning your thoughts.

"I may lose money," Mama said, "but the positive outcome of moving forward will far outweigh any real estate loss I might take."

You're back, Mama! For the next few months, twice a day, Mama sat on the couch, reading her "T" chart out loud, her ideal buyer statement, and her bold prediction, visualizing everything coming true. For the time being, Mama seemed to have moved through her feelings of despair, abandonment, and failure, past her worry about bankruptcy—but she needed to remain diligent to keep her optimistic outlook. Coco hoped Mama would stick to her routine. She pictured it every day, all day. It would be tough—too little income, too many bills, and, of course, both of them to feed, but she knew it would all work out.

Early one Sunday, a week before Christmas, the phone rang while Mama, barely awake, was pouring coffee and filling Coco's water bowl. Mama had come down with a bad winter cold and was having a hard time staying positive. "Who the hell is calling this early?" Mama grumbled. It was the realtor, with news of a couple who'd spotted the *For Sale* sign while driving past. They had requested a showing later in the day, the realtor said.

"Thank goodness we put the Christmas tree up before I got sick," Mama said. "I'd better get going." She dragged on her winter coat. Pulled her hat over her hair. Tugged on thick gloves. Sighed. Slowly wound her scarf around her neck. Bent over to pull on snow boots. Swore. Stripped off her gloves to apply ChapStick, then grabbed the gloves again. It was snowing heavily, and she hated having to go outside.

"I'll be back in a bit," she told Coco, and trudged out to shovel six inches of snow from the driveway. She worked for an hour—stopping every few minutes to lean on the shovel—until the driveway was clear and huge piles of snow banked each side. Leaning on her shovel, Mama looked back toward the house and spotted Coco, watching over her, worrying about her out in the cold, and also keeping an eye on things in general. Mama smiled and lifted her hand, a weak wave. Coco loved seeing her happy. *The driveway looks good,* Coco thought. *Now Mama can take a nap before the realtor comes.*

Around four o'clock, Mama came out from the bedroom, dressed up and ready to show the house. She pulled cookie dough from the fridge, scooped tablespoons of the mixture onto a baking sheet, and slid the pan into the oven. When the cookies were done, Mama set them out on one of her Christmas plates, and then she set the stage. With the fire blazing, jazz playing through surround sound, she and Coco sat on the couch to wait for the possible buyers. Mama was so sick, she could barely move, but when the doorbell rang, she was so excited, she jumped up to answer.

I'm outta here. Coco took off, hiding behind the couch as she watched Mama throw open the door and welcome the visitors. The minute they crossed the threshold, their faces lit up. Their names were Beth and Larry. They felt familiar to Coco, like she'd known them for years, almost like family.

"Almost" being the operative word. She'd rather stay behind the couch, but Coco went in to help entertain. She wanted to sell this house!

Mama, Beth, and Larry nibbled on cookies and sipped cocktails instead of coffee. It was more like a party than a house showing. After two hours and many happy words, Mama said goodbye, shut the door behind Beth and Larry, and dropped onto the couch. Coco jumped on her lap, so excited.

"Coco!" Mama said. "I just KNOW they're going to buy our house." Then, forgetting Coco, she jumped up. Coco spun and landed on her feet.

Hey! I know you have a hard time sitting still, but geez! I was just getting comfortable!

"I'm getting the 'T' chart," Mama called, and returned with the pad of paper in her hand. "Okay," she said, "let's check the profile for our ideal buyer." And sure enough, there they were. Beth and

Larry. The exact ideal buyers, ones who would appreciate all that this home provided. Coco felt happy to see Mama excited again.

"Woohoo!" Mama said. "It worked. I changed my outcome. I attracted the ideal buyer just like we created! Classic law of attraction!"

Woohoo is right! Coco was so happy for Mama. She'd been clear on her vision, on what she'd wanted to manifest. She'd had faith in her vision, and that had helped her move forward. Coco had never dreamed that she would have had to remind Mama of the very things that Mama had taught her, but now the roles were reversed, and she was so very happy she could help.

BECOME MORE:

- Focus on clarifying what you DO want rather than what you DON'T. Frame your goals in a positive light with specific language.

- Say to yourself, "I'm in the process of becoming or finding (fill in the blank) versus, "I don't want to be (fill in the blank). For example, "I'm in the process of finding the ideal company to work for in the field of marketing." This is a great start to manifest your dream job versus saying, "I don't want to work in a cubicle without windows like my parents." The Universe cannot differentiate between DO or DON'T so focus on what you WANT.

CHAPTER NINE
ONE LIFE—TRANSITION

BETH AND LARRY, the perfect buyers, bid too low, and by February, after two months of forced cheer, Mama gave it up, slid into depression, and hit rock bottom.

"I have two choices," Mama said to Coco while slumped over the dining room table, staring at the pile of bills on the table before her. "(A) Sell the house or (B) Declare bankruptcy."

Coco meowed. *Surely we could get creative.*

"Yeah," Mama said. "I'm with you. (A) seems to be a no-go."

That's sooo not what I said! She was so frustrated. Mama was living in her own no-win world. She had completely shut down to possibilities, which also cost Coco a life, but Coco was ready and willing to help Mama rally back at any cost. Coco then remembered Ted from years ago. In an oddly similar way, Mama was just like him, but she was stuck on the ledge in her mind. Coco was afraid Mama was paralyzed with fear, unable to see any positive outcomes, causing her own negative spiral to continue. *What if you can't turn the corner, Mama? Will you leave me?*

Mama took a sip of coffee.

Coco jumped onto Mama's lap and curled up. Mama scratched between her ears. *Once? One scratch? That's it? Really?*

Peering into her coffee cup, Mama said, her voice flat, "I have to take action."

Coco bumped her head against Mama's stomach. *Let's do it. Anything!* Mama didn't move. Coco bumped again. "Crap," Mama said, sloshing her coffee on the table.

What could we do? Coco lifted her head, Mama's black robe smooth under her paws. She'd have to risk a headache and try to send Mama pictures again. She envisioned Mama holding her phone and Beth and Larry holding theirs. *Pick up the phone and call their realtor, Mama.*

Mama squinted her eyes, then opened them, as if to focus. "I wish Beth and Larry would just call with a higher offer. That would solve everything."

Oh, boy. This could take all day. She'd just have to keep trying. Coco closed her eyes and pictured Mama punching out numbers on her phone.

"Or I could call them, I guess."

Ding ding ding ding! Now you're thinking Mama!

"Who am I kidding?" Mama said. "Nobody does that. I'll look too desperate—Ow! Coco! You just nipped me! What's up with you?"

I have to get serious. Mama needs help NOW.

It was almost time for her mid-morning snack. What would she have? Pouncies, her favorite treat? Fish or chicken? It was so hard to choose. Her nostrils twitched just thinking of Mama tearing open the bag, that amazing smell, the velvety texture, taste buds zinging… she was definitely off-topic. Coco willed Mama to look at her. Mama had taught her that changing her thoughts and beliefs would change her outcome, and that she could attract more of what she wanted. *Mama needs to remember that.* She had seen herself jumping to the top of the cabinet, learned that the geese couldn't get to her through the glass, realized that the horrific beast she thought was out to kill her was just a fuzzy, smelly D.O.G. who only wanted to play.

Mama shifted in her chair, sat up a little straighter. "Screw protocol," Mama said, then out of nowhere, looking surprised, she said, "Coco, time for me to pick up the damn phone."

Yay! Mama gets it! Now let's celebrate with Pouncies!

🐾 🐾

Larry and Beth's realtor hadn't answered, so Mama left a message. After she'd hung up, Mama went into the living room, snapped open her briefcase, and pulled out a pen and a notebook. She stepped over Coco, who was pacing in front of the coffee table, and sat back on the couch. Across the top of the pad, she printed *BOLD PREDICTION.*

"Let me try something, Coco." She clicked the pen. Click. Click.

She'd been going on about the bold prediction for months. Mama seemed to be all talk and no action about all things bold prediction, but maybe she was taking action now. The prediction said that whatever money Mama might lose would multiply by one hundred and would be her annual net worth some day. So why hadn't Mama put anything forth? Maybe she was scared.

Click. Click. There she went with the pen again.

Coco jumped on the couch, curled up next to Mama and purred.

"How about this?" Mama asked. "I'm saying this out loud, Coco. Stating it loud and clear. Here we go. Whatever money I might lose on this house times one hundred will be my annual net income some day." Coco purred. Mama seemed much happier when she said those words, so Coco was definitely behind the bold prediction.

Mama was thinking and doodling. Coco saw her scribbling the number 11 on the first page of the notebook. Her favorite number. She'd been talking for the past few years about growing her business to $11 million a year. Coco was all for that. Eleven million would buy her truckloads of Q-tips and toys.

Besides, she would do whatever she could to help Mama. One of the financial people Mama liked to watch on TV always said how much easier it was to make financial sacrifices if you knew you'd see an increase in earnings later. She stressed how important it was to see money as more fluid, not a security blanket to cling to at all costs. Mama needed to remember those words.

Mama reached for her calculator and punched in $110,000, the amount of the loss between what Mama owed on the house, the penalty and taxes to cash out of her IRA early, and the amount Beth and Larry were willing to pay. Then she could toss the keys over and get them back in their condo. "I hate this, Coco," Mama sighed. "I eat $110,000. I lose, and they get what they want—our house. Cheap."

Of course, Coco thought, *we'll get what we want most too. We can move back into our condo, which we love. We can leave this huge house full of memories that just make you sad, Mama.* Coco snuggled next to Mama.

"Okay," Mama said, "let's see how this plays out." She did the math on her calculator. "Holy crap," Mama said. "The net worth— it's $11 million, my target number. How could I have not seen that?" And then she started crying, wiping her eyes with the back of her hand. "I got a 'Yes' from the Universe," she said. "I eat it now, but later, the Universe is telling me 'Yes.' I asked for a sign and this is HUGE!"

Mama reached for Coco, pulling her from her cozy nest, her hands gripping Coco behind her front legs, while Coco, put out but wanting to show support, hung there, suspended above the couch, hanging like a ragdoll, tolerating the hug. *Is this for real? Mama seems reinvigorated so that's gotta be good!*

Seven weeks to the hour after Mama had calculated the total for her bold prediction, she waltzed into her realtor's office to meet with the title company, her realtor, and the buyer's realtor. The house value was underwater, and she had to pay the difference with all of her retirement fund, but the weight was lifted! Armed with that big check of nearly her entire life's savings, the keys, and a huge smile, she freed herself. The ordeal was over. Mama's hard work had paid off. Resilience! Faith! Taking action had paid off! Mama hadn't actually labeled the $110,000 as a loss, but rather as an investment—not the Suze Orman kind of investment, but the one called 'cutting your losses.'

🐾 🐾

After they sold their house, Mama and Coco moved back to their condo, where Coco spent hours sitting wide-eyed, taking it all in. *Home.* It took almost 7 years but Mama rallied back from near bankruptcy to a thriving business, and she was the first to acknowledge that without Coco, the outcome could have been very different. They were happy, content, and, after a few months, Coco knew her work was done and she became gravely ill. Mama had taught her everything, and then, as she'd moved through half her lives, she'd been able to return the favor, watching out for Mama, helping her. Coco had lived her lives to the fullest, and at age 16, Coco was ready to transition to a greater role, one much higher and loftier than ever before. True, she was a little cat, but she had an infinite soul, and she'd always watch over Mama.

She had lots of wisdom to share with the world too, to help make it a more positive place. *Where should I start?* Should she rid the world of smelly beasts—the ones that fetched and rolled over? *Well, they are kind of fun to chase and hiss at, so maybe not.* She was sure she could find other things to do. *Now that I know how... what am I waiting for?*

❧ ❧

In heaven, Coco has perfectly trimmed claws. Mama would be happy to know that. In heaven, she can climb trees. There's one tree she loves. It's got all kinds of winding branches, crisscrossing, so she can jump or step from limb to limb, no matter where she is on the tree. She never has to worry that she won't be able to get down. It's a tree of staircases. She loves going up there. And the leaves, they smell so good. Sharp, really sharp, and fresh. They even smell green. Smelling is one of Coco's favorite things to do.

In heaven, Coco plays with geese. She doesn't need a glass door to feel safe. She loves them. They play every day. She waits, watches, and then springs. They run and flap their wings—swirls of white and gray and air on her face every time. She used to be afraid of those wings, but not now. Sometimes the geese come at her like they're going to peck at her, and she twirls. She's amazing. She pretends to sink her claws into a wing. She jumps back, arches her back, and hisses! They take off. They honk.

In heaven, Coco watches Mama. Her job is just to play, but she still looks out for Mama. The other day, Mama was crying. Coco wasn't sure why. It wasn't because of poor sales performance. Mama didn't have to cry about that. Her sales were fantastic. Coco couldn't jump down to her and curl up on her lap and purr, so instead, she put a picture in Mama's head about when Mama had made a video of her jumping to the top cabinet, then showed it to everyone on Facebook. And then Mama smiled. Coco put another picture in her head of her watching Mama from the Rainbow Bridge, with her ears twitching—that's cat talk to humans, in pictures—and Coco knew Mama understood, because she said out loud, wiping her eyes, "You little weasel. I'll be okay. I learned so much from you!"

Well, weasel wasn't Coco's actual name, but Mama had liked to call her that, and Coco had let her, because it had made Mama happy. Besides, it *was* her nickname, just like Mama's was Queenie. And being Queenie's daughter made Coco a part of royalty. *I AM royalty and don't you forget it!*

Heaven was the beginning of a new world for Coco. *I have a lot more to share. This is JUST the beginning!*

BECOME MORE:

- Reframe a seemingly awful situation by focusing on what's going right rather than what's going wrong.

- The Law of Attraction states that you will receive more of what you focus upon. Therefore, if you think/obsess about debt, the more debt you'll attract. Why not think about attracting prosperity, bonuses, projects, opportunities, girlfriends, boyfriends, and JOY? The positive momentum of your thoughts alone will start to bring them to you! The amount of time until you manifest them is balanced with the doubt you feel deep within yourself. Think about that!

- Helping others grow in their personal journey is the ultimate gift you can give.

CONCLUSION

THE MESSAGE

THE PROFESSOR FINISHED speaking, paused, and looked up at his audience. Hands shot up. He pointed to a woman in the first row.

"I can't believe Coco died!" the woman said, her voice cracking. "Was she sick for long? What happened?"

The professor raised an eyebrow. "*Did* she die? That's the real question. Yes, the vet put her down—it was emotionally unbearable, as Mama held Coco tight in her blanket, which was her initial reference to me that *yes she faced death* with the purest love of her life. Brave little Coco became ill—but she is more alive than ever, bigger than life, and sharing her story." The professor cleared his throat. He wasn't used to making his point by talking about cats, but he felt Coco and his former student had huge lessons to teach.

"As I shared this story with you, illustrating Coco's vast personal growth throughout her journey, describing her incredible bond with Mama, I wanted you to recognize that each of us has a responsibility to ourselves to question past beliefs, to ask the question: Does this serve me?"

"We also have a responsibility to recognize that the words we use have an immense impact on us and on others around us—our families, our friends, our colleagues."

"For some people, it takes a lifetime for them to realize how deeply their inner thoughts have impacted their lives. They carried the burden of false beliefs because someone told them they could not do this or achieve that—and they believed it! It is only once they release those thoughts by asking, "Says who?" can they finally start on the path to gain a sense of their authentic self, freed from the hurts and misconceptions that have plagued them throughout their lives. These are the brick walls that have stopped them from having meaningful relationships, careers they love, and living with the feeling they are serving the world with a purpose."

"This lack of authenticity starts when we believe someone else's perception of who we really are. It eats away at our self-esteem until we reframe our thoughts, our words and our actions of what we really want, gaining clarity and focus along the way. I want you to know that regardless of what age you are, you have a choice to be the master of your own happiness, to not rely on others to fill that void or blame outside circumstances for where you are today."

"Many people are afraid of becoming their vulnerable selves, to allow their unique differences to be seen, and to shine like Coco. Corporate America is losing out on the huge asset that authenticity provides, but as you enter the workforce, it's up to you to be brave and force this paradigm shift."

"Let me ask all of you, how different would our economy be if you were a part of a workforce that is incredibly passionate about what you sell or build or create? A workforce where every person collectively uses their imagination or vision as a team to create the momentum to accomplish great things? A place where you focus on "what can be" versus "it can't be done."

Immediately, a graduate shouted, "I want to work for a company like that!"

"Me too!" yelled a woman from the back. "So are these the words I should say to myself to help me focus on the ideal work environment?"

The professor smiled and said, "One of my favorite questions I ask myself is what problem or issue can I solve today? Or how do I want the world to be different?" A more philosophical mindset would quote Gandhi, "Be the change you wish to see in the world."

"So you tell me, my friend… is that what you want?" the professor asked the woman in the back. "If so, you are leaps and bounds ahead of so many who never asked themselves what they really want, wasting precious time that could last a lifetime."

"Many people squander months and years of their lives sleepwalking, divorced from their true selves. And if we don't know how much we are capable of, we cannot form clear ideas and use the power of our minds to impact our lives and the world around us."

"Here's another question: Did you ever find yourself doubting your true talent because one teacher or coach or fellow student questioned that talent?"

Many of the graduates looked around the room. A few raised their hands.

"C'mon now," the professor said. "It's not *you* who should be embarrassed or ashamed."

Slowly, hands started to go up, stopping halfway, seemingly unwilling to be seen.

From the back of the auditorium, the control booth door squeaked open, casting a dim light on the seats in the back row, startling several members of the audience, and causing a minor interruption. Three people—the same three the producer had yelled at earlier, cussing them out, calling them incompetent—stood on the landing. One by one, they raised their hands high in the air.

The professor, realizing the potential power of these people's stories, asked the three if they would like to join him on stage. They looked at each other, nervous. One of the men, the one in the green t-shirt, looked at the floor, the other two whispered to each other. Someone in the audience started a slow clap of which others soon followed, urging the three to come forward.

The other man, in the baseball cap, hesitated, then turned and began to walk down the stairs. His colleague, the woman in charge of audio, followed, reaching for his hand. As she grasped it, she turned around, and extended her other hand to the man in the green t-shirt, who reluctantly took it. The three descended the stairs. With each step and each clap from the audience, they held their heads higher, their strides became more confident. By the time they descended the stairs to the stage, the noise was deafening, graduates jumping to their feet, everyone clapping wildly.

The professor greeted the crew members one by one, shaking their hands and then pulling each one in for a hug. Several audience members were moved to tears.

The professor allowed the audience to continue their frenzied applause and urged the trio to face the standing ovation they were receiving. The man with the baseball cap nodded his head and cleared his throat nervously as his eyes welled with gratitude at the warm response from the audience. He and his crew always worked behind the scenes, invisible to the audience. To receive such acknowledgement felt incredible.

After several minutes passed, the audience settled down and the professor asked the three, "What triggered you to walk out of that sound booth and participate in this session?"

The woman reached for the microphone and cleared her throat. She shook visibly but clearly wanted to answer the question.

"You know what happened, Professor. You were there when my boss blew up."

"Yes, I was. Would you mind sharing what happened with our audience?"

"Okay," she said. "I'll try to summarize. Just as you started speaking and said you wouldn't need your PowerPoint presentation, my producer went ballistic. He was already furious because we hadn't yet wired you for sound when you were about to go on stage. What he didn't realize was that the mic pack *he* had handed to me needed a new battery—we were in the process of getting a replacement. We did not want it to go dead midway through your speech. He berated me in front of everyone, including you. I knew it was getting close to your stage time, but damn it, I had it covered!"

"How did that make you feel?" the professor asked.

"Worthless. Stupid. Insignificant. Angry… is that enough? After how he treated me, I lost so much respect for him because I lost respect for my own talent. Quite frankly, I was already writing my resignation email in my head."

"How could it have been different?" the professor asked.

"He could have said in a normal tone, 'Is there a problem? Do you have a Plan B? How can I help?' But instead, I get chewed out in front of everyone making me question why I still work here when I can easily find another audio job down the street!"

The graduates nodded their heads. Then the professor looked toward the back of the room, pausing for effect. His expression serious, the professor asked, "Mr. Producer? Can you please join me on stage?"

The audience grew silent—not a giggle or whisper while they waited to see how the professor would handle the situation.

After what felt like a very long ten seconds, a man in the control booth, wearing a headset, barked over the loudspeaker, "I don't need to join you, Professor. You've made your point."

"Really?" the professor asked. "I beg your pardon, but I haven't even started."

The trio on the stage whispered to each other. "Oh geez, this is getting ugly," said the man in the baseball cap.

"Fine," the professor said. "I'll join YOU." The professor then walked down the three steps at stage left and proceeded to the staircase that formed the center aisle of the first tier of seats in the auditorium.

The producer opened the squeaky door of the control booth, stepped out, and slammed it behind him, showing himself to the audience for the first time. He stood watching as the professor continued up the stairs. "I'm happy to meet you halfway," the professor said, though the producer was not budging from his place by the control booth.

As the professor stopped at the precise middle of the auditorium, in the mezzanine section, a single spotlight focused on him. The professor looked around from this new perspective above the stage. "I ask again, would you be willing to meet me halfway?"

With apprehension, his light blue polo drenched with perspiration, the producer exhaled loudly, and proceeded slowly down a few stairs.

"I'd like to hear your side of the story before I say anything more," the professor said.

This gesture alone disarmed the producer, who started to ramble about having a bad start to his morning. "It's been a shit week altogether," the producer said. "At home… and then today I was late arriving here for the commencement because traffic was backed up on the interstate. I kept telling myself I don't want to work such long hours and I hate the long commute and I'm sick of doing everything around here… "

"Wow! You sure are clear about what you DON'T want" said the professor. Tell me what you DO want?

The producer bowed his head, silent.

"This is also an example of the law of attraction because the producer is focusing on what he doesn't want, and guess what, he got a lot of it," the professor said to the audience. "Unfortunately, this is why people disengage in the workforce that you are about to enter. The producer has a terrible week and has one negative thought after the other, you just heard him, and then takes his anger, fear, and frustration out on his colleagues—and everyone feels terrible, everyone wants to give up or get out. It's toxic!"

"In an extreme example, think about Ted, the man who jumped off Coco's building. Surely he didn't feel as though he had options, that he was worthwhile, that he had a community. Suicide is a very complicated topic that I cannot even pretend to understand. But think of how the situation perhaps could have been different." The professor turned to the producer. "What if you had come to your colleagues and told them you were having a really bad day? A really bad week, actually."

The professor then turned to the crew. "And what if your producer had been more open with all of you? Maybe you would have felt more empowered to make decisions in his absence and to tell him you needed a minute to fix the battery pack, but that you've got it covered."

He turned to the audience. "They could have all supported each other and worked as a team to make sure my speech went smoothly. When you communicate and treat people fairly, include them in making decisions, and allow them to independently contribute, they'll go the extra mile. When you don't do these things? They'll retreat. And if it's really severe, they will actively disengage, happy to tell the world in this case how much they dislike this university, their policies, and YOU, Mr. Producer. It's called, 'I quit.'"

The producer visibly cringed. He looked down at the stage. "I was out of line and... I'm sorry," he said to his crew. Their faces softened.

The producer walked down a few more stairs to meet the professor on the mezzanine landing. "I never realized how accountable we all are to each other," the producer said. "I need my team to make these productions run smoothly. If any one of them left, it would be a huge loss. Having them lose respect for me is my wake-up call. Funny, my wife tells me I never say I'm sorry... I assumed she just knew, but I guess words do make a difference. I better get back to the booth now," he said.

The producer shook the professor's hand and turned to walk back up the stairs to the booth. The audience was silent, moved.

"Wait," the audio woman called from the stage. "I want to say thank you. That had to be hard in front of all these people, and quite frankly it's the first time you ever apologized to any of us."

The three descended the stairs of the stage and climbed toward the control booth to get back to work.

The professor returned to the stage, and turned to the audience. "Well that turned out better than I'd predicted. So just for a minute, let's examine further how debilitating needless anger and criticism can impact our self-worth simply from the words that we hear." He drew a circle in the air. "We get into this cycle—we start to doubt ourselves, we lose our center, and we become fearful and sometimes aggressive all at once. And fear blankets our authentic talents, purpose, and beliefs. Let me ask you, if that kind of criticism came from a coach or teacher, would it help you to do better? Would it fire you up to make positive changes?"

"Are you kidding?" someone yelled. "I second-guessed myself into a really negative place."

"It became a self-fulfilling prophecy," shouted another. "I couldn't see my way out."

"I only wanted to hear someone say, 'I'm sorry' after they barked at me," another graduate called. "Sometimes people get angry, I understand that, but we have to be accountable and have a human moment when they do!"

"Exactly," the professor said. "That direct feedback may work when we actively request it, but when coupled with a less-than-positive tone and attitude, the majority of us end up mistrusting ourselves. We end up hiding anything about ourselves that's unique, anything that makes us stand out. Take Coco. She struggled with that tail of hers. She was proud of it. She was embarrassed by it. She learned to love it. It was lopped off. She had to reframe. In the end, that tail served her well. She learned a lot of life lessons from her tail."

"We all have a curly-bent tail we struggle with. What's yours?

What quality do you have that you're sensitive about or have been criticized for that you can turn into your key differentiator? If you can take only one thing from this entire story, take this—honor what makes you unique. Honor yourself. Look into the mirror and say, I am worthy."

"In closing, I'd like to take a look at the big picture of the workforce that you are about to enter. There's a huge shift going on. We're living in a time of accelerated change, a paradigm shift. Are people and businesses more interested in staying with the status quo? No, because if they do, they're not going to grow. They're going to be left behind."

"Think about how exciting work would be if every day you felt as though you were truly contributing, that you were collaborating with others to create game-changing solutions? Pretty great, right? Think about how amazing it would be to realize that same model outside the workplace as well. You've seen what Coco went through and what Mama went through, and how they helped each other with thoughts becoming things. Are you ready to live an authentic life? To become more?"

Heads were nodding, "Yes!" "Yes!" "Yes!"

Then, on the far right of the auditorium, a well-dressed female stood up from her seat, dabbing her eyes with a Kleenex. The lighting technician in the control booth noticed her immediately and focused a single spotlight on her as she raised her hand. The professor, locking eyes with the woman, realized it was her—his former student! The professor held out his hand to give her the floor.

She scanned the audience, then simply said, "What *are* we waiting for?"

ABOUT THE AUTHOR

Nancy West was born selling.

In first grade, after growing tired of her classmates constantly asking to "borrow" a pencil, she started renting them for a nickel a day. She proudly secured her "inventory" in Crown Royal's signature velvet bag and jingled her earnings in her lunch box on the school bus every day.

Encouraged by her parents to embrace her entrepreneurial spirit, Nancy went on to complete her undergraduate and graduate studies at night, earning high honors, at the same time establishing herself as one of the top female sales representatives in the transportation industry.

After recovering from a layoff, Nancy found herself thriving in sales in the corporate training industry. Inspired to blend her sales savvy with her newly discovered talent for facilitating and coaching, Nancy then went on to build her own consultancy, Accelerated Performance, Inc. Today she works with many of the biggest brands in the automotive industry, training salespeople in car showrooms from coast to coast.

Equal to her passion for cars, is her love of guiding the youngest generation entering the workforce. In this, her first book, she transforms the most difficult lessons from her own life into stories that encourage the release of self-limiting beliefs and promote action.

Originally from Ohio, Nancy has called several suburbs of Detroit home for over 20 years and now resides in beautiful Bloomfield Hills, MI. When she isn't on the road, she can be found indulging her passion for home remodeling, cooking, and gardening.

NANCY **M** WEST
BECOME MORE

For more information visit www.NancyMWest.com.

ABOUT COCO

A portion of the profit from this book will be dedicated
to helping shelter cats find their forever home.

Playful And Wise Stuff

So you finished my book and I bet you're thinking, "Wow... I never knew kitties could be so smart?" Surprise!

Sure I might be a little cat, but I have LOTS of wisdom to share! Sign up for your weekly dose of PAWS (Playful and Wise Stuff) to keep you purring! It's free and you can unsubscribe anytime... and I promise I won't hiss!

Visit
http://nancymwest.com/paws-from-coco-with-love/

With Love,
Coco 🐾

www.ingramcontent.com/pod-product-compliance
Lightning Source LLC
Chambersburg PA
CBHW070707190326
41458CB00004B/887